New Office Technology

Human and Organizational Aspects

New Office Technology

Human and Organizational Aspects

edited by
Harry J. Otway
and
Malcolm Peltu

Ⓐ Ablex Publishing Corporation

EUR 8289
Copyright © 1983 ECSC, EEC, EAEC, Brussels and Luxembourg

Printed in Great Britain

Library of Congress Cataloging in Publication Data
Otway, Harry J., 1935
New Office Technology

Bibliography: P.
Includes index.
1. Office practice-Automation-Addresses, Essays, Lectures.
I. Peltu, M. (Malcolm)   II. Title.
HF5547.5.0'87   1983   651.8'4   82-24473

ISBN 0-89391-198-4

Legal Notice
Neither the Commission of the European Communities nor any person acting on
behalf of the Commission is responsible for the use which might be made of the
following information.

TABLE OF CONTENTS

THE EDITORS

Harry J. Otway is Head of Technology Assessment in the Informatics, Mathematics and Systems Analysis Department of the European Communities Joint Research Centre at Ispra, Italy and is responsible for the INSIS Human and Organizational Aspects functions; he joined the Commission from the International Institute of Applied Systems Analysis (IIASA), near Vienna. He has a long-standing and varied interest in the policy issues arising from the interaction between technical and social systems. He has published extensively and has been a consultant to governments and international agencies and a visiting professor at several major universities.

Malcolm Peltu is an information technology consultant and journalist. He became a computing professional in 1965 and has extensive experience of the technology. In 1972 he started working as a journalist. He has been editor of one of Europe's leading technical newspapers, *Computer Weekly;* computer consultant to *New Scientist;* and London Correspondent of the US publication *Datamation*. He specializes in interpreting the technology to the layman and has written three books, *A Guide to the Electronic Office* (Associated Business Publishers, 1981), *Introducing Computers* (National Computing Centre, 1982) and *Using Computers — A Manager's Guide* (National Computing Centre, 1981).

THE AUTHORS

André Danzin (Chapter 1) is Chairman of the Sub-committee on Research and Development in Informatics and Information Technology of the European Committee for Research in Science and Technology (CREST) and is a Special Adviser to the Commission of the European Community on the industrial and social impact of information technologies. He was formerly Vice President and General Manager of the leading French electronics firm Thomson-CSF and has been director of France's foremost centre for research into computer-related activities, IRIA. He has published studies which indicate how informatics could lead to a new industrial renaissance.

Anthony G. Hopwood (Chapter 2) is the Institute of Chartered Accountants' Professor of Accounting and Financial Reporting at the London Graduate School of Business Studies. He also serves as visiting Professor of Management at the European Institute for Advanced Studies in Management, Brussels, and in 1981 was nominated to serve as the American Accounting Association's Distinguished International Visiting Professor in the USA. The human, organizational and social dimensions of accounting, information and control systems provide the focus of his research and consultancy work. He is Editor-in-Chief of the international research journal, *Accounting, Organizations, and Society.*

Peter G. W. Keen (Chapter 3) is Chairman of Micro Mainframe Inc. in Cambridge, Massachusetts, USA. He has held faculty positions at the Sloan School of Management at Massachusetts Institute of Technology, and at Stanford, Wharton and Harvard Universities and is a consultant to private and public sector organizations in the USA, Europe and Latin America. His main research and teaching interest has been in Decision Support Systems (DSS), education, the management of organizational change, and telecommunications policy. He has written many articles and publications and is editor of the journal *Office: Technology and People* and Consulting Editor for the Addison-Wesley series on Decision Support and its Micro-DSS series software.

8

Enid Mumford (Chapter 4) has carried out extensive practical research into the impact of technology on people at the workplace. She is Professor of Organizational Behaviour at the Manchester Business School, where she has developed a participative design methodology aimed at assisting users of technology to play an influential role in shaping the way technology affects the working environment. She has also made special studies of industrial relations problems on the docks and in coal mining. She is the author of eighteen books and numerous articles.

Michel Crozier (Chapter 5) has a worldwide reputation as a perceptive sociologist and writer. He is Senior Research Professor at the Centre National de la Recherche Scientifique (CNRS) and Director of the Centre de Sociologie des Organisations, a research institute which is part of CNRS. He has travelled throughout the world, is a frequent visiting professor at Harvard University in the USA, and has been a consultant to many organizations, including the Rand Corporation, the Commission of the European Communities and various centres in Europe dedicated to management training. He has published seven books which have been widely read.

Federico Butera (Chapter 6) has participated in many large projects involving the design of organizational systems which incorporate new technology. He is the founder and director of RSO, the Institute of Action Research and Organization in Milan and frequently acts as a consultant to the International Labour Organization and the European Foundation for the Improvement of Living and Working Conditions. Previously, he was director of Olivetti's Centre for Sociological Research and Organizational Studies. *Emilio Bartezzaghi* is an electronic engineering graduate who specializes in organization and management in the Dipartimento di Elettronica at Milan Polytechnic. He provides research, teaching and consulting services in the design of organization and information systems for RSO.

Niels Bjørn-Andersen (Chapter 7) is an Associate Professor in the multidisciplinary Information Systems Research Group at the Copenhagen School of Economics and Business Administration. He has specialized in the design of information systems and their impact on the work roles of clerks and managers. He gained his doctorate for the study of Decision Support Systems and has written many books and articles on how to implement a participative form of systems design which takes into account social, organizational and psychological aspects. He has been a visiting researcher at Manchester Business School and visiting professor at Paris University IX Dauphine.

Brian Wynne (Chapter 8) is a lecturer at the multidisciplinary School of Independent Studies, University of Lancaster, UK. His professional research has concentrated mainly on policy issues relating to technology and science. He has acted as a consultant on large-scale technology projects. In 1981 he was a visiting scientist at the Commission of the European Communities' Joint Research Centre in Ispra, Italy, in 1983 a project leader at IIASA, near Vienna. He has published extensively in the fields of technological politics and sociology of scientific knowledge.

John Evans (Chapter 9) has made a special study of international industrial and Research and Development policies. He is Research Officer for the European Trade Union Institute in Brussels and was previously Industrial Secretary at the International Federation of Commercial Clerical and Technical Employees (FIET), based in Geneva. He graduated with a degree in Philosophy, Politics and Economics at Oxford University and worked in the Economics Department of the British Trade Union Congress for five years. His publications include many reports on employment and industrial policies and he was one of the authors of a Club of Rome study on microelectronics and society, published in 1982.

Albert Armbruster (Chapter 10) is a professor at the Technical University of Berlin. His responsibility at the University's Institute for Industrial Engineering is to conduct research into the physiological and ergonomic aspects of equipment and work design. He has specialized in the application of new technology to administration and office work. Before joining the Technical University in 1964 as a chief engineer, he worked in the Department of Industrial Engineering at a leading computing and electronics company, Siemens. Prior to that, he was at the Institute of Physiology at the Free University of Berlin.

Sigurd Jensen (Chapter 11) is engaged in research projects and consulting services at the Department of Industrial Psychology in the Technological Institute, Tåstrup, Denmark. He specializes in the analysis of psychological and physiological impacts of advanced technology on job content and working conditions, particularly in relation to office work and to automated production in process industries. He is the author of several works on these subjects, including being co-author of two reports on the working environment at visual display terminals, published by the European Foundation for the Improvement of Living and Working Conditions.

Jacques Hebenstreit (Chapter 12) won the Annual Award in Computer Science of the French Academy of Sciences in 1980 in recognition of his contribution to the development of computing and educational policies. He is a professor of Computer Science at the Ecole Supérieure d'Electricité and chairman of the Technical Committee of the International Federation for Information Processing (IFIP). He is a member of two national committees in France concerned with informatics in university and secondary school education and was on the Programme Committee of the Third World Conference on Computers in Education in 1981. He is the author of over fifty papers and articles and a consultant on computer-assisted education for UNESCO.

Rob Kling (Chapter 13) is an Associate Professor of Information and Computer Science and at the University of California, Irvine, USA. He is Chairman of an International Federation for Information Processing (IFIP) Working Group on the Social Accountability of Computing and is Editor of the Department on the Social Impacts of Computing of the *Communications of the ACM*. His current research focuses on studies of the use and impacts of computing in organizations and policy issues relating to new computing technologies, such as electronic funds transfer. He has consulted on the appropriate development and use of computerized technologies with several governments and private firms.

ACKNOWLEDGEMENTS

The editors are indebted to many people, especially Hans Jørgen Helms and John Peters. Without their personal commitment and continuing support neither the workshop nor this book would have been possible. They are also grateful to their INSIS colleagues who helped in varying ways. It is impossible to list them all but mention should be made of Michel Audoux, Garth Davies, Anthony Dunning, Cornelis Jansen van Rosendaal, Marcel Mesnage, Edward Phillips, Jean-Pierre Valentin, Joep van der Veer and all members of sub-group IV. Ria Volcan, Megan Jones and Andrea Broom handled the mountains of paperwork with good cheer and efficiency.

The editors are, of course, indebted to the contributors who mostly met deadlines and usually wrote on the topics they had been assigned. They all patiently tolerated extensive editing and rewriting of their prose, making individual sacrifices in the interest of having a uniform style and better continuity of their combined efforts.

FOREWORD

The production and use of information technologies will be a major source of economic growth and social development into the twenty-first century. In order to ensure that the benefits of the technology are fully harnessed to the well-being of all aspects of society, the Council, Member State governments and Commission of the European Communities are committed to a strategy for the 'information age' that blends social and political goals with economic and industrial imperatives. An important manifestation of this commitment is the *I*nter-institutional i*N*tegrated *S*ervices *I*nformation *S*ystem, known by its abbreviation, INSIS. This is a programme consisting of a strategic action plan within which co-ordinated projects are being initiated to introduce advanced office technology and communications services into public institutions and representative bodies from the EEC and its Member States.

When introducing new technology, there is always a temptation to try to gain the potential benefits as quickly as possible. The experience of many users of computer-based systems clearly indicates that these benefits will fail to materialize if inadequate consideration is given to the broad impact of new systems on all aspects of the user environment. The analysis and forecasting of actual user needs therefore lies at the heart of the process leading to the achievement of the main INSIS goals.

INSIS has specific objectives for stimulating the implementation of advanced information systems within the EEC and the growth of European information technology and information industries. It will also make an important contribution to the general development of information services that improve the efficiency of organizations at the same time as improving the quality of working environments and the job satisfaction of individuals working within them.

The Commission and the INSIS management team hope that this book will be a step in the process of creating a framework that will allow potentially revolutionary changes in the way people work and live to proceed at a manageable, evolutionary pace. We believe that exciting new office technologies will be translated into effective services only if human and organizational aspects are given the same amount of care and priority as the technical design. It is gratifying that such distinguished contributors agreed to work closely with Dr Otway and Mr Peltu in the continuing framework of INSIS to produce this important publication.

John Peters,
Chief Advisor,
Secretariat-General,
Commission of the
European Communities,
Brussels, Belgium.

Hans Jørgen Helms
Director,
Informatics, Mathematics and
Systems Analysis Department,
Commission of the
European Communities,
Joint Research Centre,
Ispra, Italy.

INTRODUCTION

In 1900, less than 20 per cent of the labour force in industrialized countries worked in offices. Now, over 50 per cent of those employed are 'white-collar' office staff and the proportion is rising. Until the mid-1970s, when small business computers and word processors were introduced, office technology had hardly changed since the turn of the century, by which time typewriters and telephones were already in use. Automatic telephone exchanges, telex, photocopiers, accounting machines and calculators made some impact on office methods, but at a far slower rate than did the rapid technological innovations in the manufacturing and agricultural sectors.

In the 1960s, large data processing computers began to carry out many office tasks, such as preparing and calculating accounts and payrolls. These systems had to be kept in specially air conditioned rooms and had little direct impact on the office environment, except that a great deal of office work became concerned with collecting information for computers or analyzing the printed reports disgorged by the machines. The 'micro chip revolution' of the mid-1970s had a dramatic effect on computer-based systems, enabling more computing capability to be packed into a smaller space and at a much reduced cost. This provided the stimulus for the development of new computer-based information technologies which are radically altering how people work in offices, and the very nature of organizations and management processes.

This new office technology, variously known as *office automation, the electronic office, office of the future* and *bureautique,* is described by André Danzin in Chapter 1. As he explains, what the technology does is more important than how it does it. The remainder of the book is therefore an examination of what new office technology could mean for the way organizations function and the working lives of white-collar staff.

Many computer-based systems have failed because senior management and systems designers have focused too much attention on technical and short-term economic objectives while under-rating, or completely ignoring, crucial social, individual and longer-term economic requirements. By looking at some of these failures, Anthony Hopwood in Chapter 2 provides advice on how to identify and evaluate the *real* benefits.

The specification, design, development, introduction, operation and maintenance of new office systems is likely to be a complex task, of central importance to the effectiveness and efficiency of an organization. Peter Keen in Chapter 3 examines how to initiate and successfully carry through office technology projects within a flexible strategic plan.

Designing an information system is concerned essentially with the design of jobs, organizational structures, inter-group and inter-personal relationships. Enid Mumford in Chapter 4 provides the background to the main traditions of systems design. She suggests an approach which will combine human and organizational aims with technical and economic objectives. In Chapter 5, Michel Crozier examines in more detail the effect of these new systems on the ability of organizations to adapt to, and survive in, evolving environments. Federico Butera and Emilio Bartezzaghi in Chapter 6 give guidelines on how to use systematic techniques in analyzing and creating the right organizational environment to make the best use of new technology.

Various groups of office staff will be affected in different ways. In Chapter 7, Niels Bjørn-Andersen looks at the impact on secretaries and clerks, which are the job roles where systems like word processors have the most impact. Managers and professional staff, however, represent a greater cost to an organization and the greatest number of office personnel. Advanced office systems are also aimed at these categories and Brian Wynne, in Chapter 8, looks at the changing roles of managers. The process of technological innovation in the office is closely allied to broader labour relations and personnel policy issues, such as the quality of the working environment, job security, staff grading procedures, training and working hours. John Evans in Chapter 9 describes the ways in which agreements have been negotiated to determine how technological change takes place.

It is important to develop systems which make the most satisfying, healthy and effective match between the needs of the person using the system and the technology. Albert Armbruster in Chapter 10 offers guidelines on the physical ergonomic equipment standards which should be met. In Chapter 11, Sigurd Jensen discusses the human requirements in the interactions between the user and the system, and the user's psychological reactions to the system.

The job roles and equipment which characterize the new office environment create a rapidly changing demand for new skills, with implications for the whole educational and training system, as well as for specific vocational tasks. Jacques Hebenstreit in Chapter 12 explores these new skill requirements, and how and where they can be met.

Rob Kling in Chapter 13 places organizational requirements in a broader social context and summarizes the main themes developed earlier in the book.

WHO SHOULD READ THIS BOOK?

This book is about people and organizations, rather than about technology. It avoids technical and sociological jargon, explaining any specialist terms that need to be used. A wide range of readers should therefore find the book interesting and useful.

Practical advice is offered for those directly involved in making decisions about and implementing new office information systems — senior executives, managers, professionals, administrators, trade unionists, staff representatives, information technology specialists and other office personnel. It will also be of value to researchers, academics and students in relevant social science and technical disciplines because the editors and authors are in the forefront of research in their specializations.

THE GENESIS OF THE BOOK

The INSIS management recognized very early on that human and organizational aspects must be given careful attention if the potential benefits of the new information technologies are to be realized (see Foreword). Accordingly, this book was conceived in the spring of 1981 when an INSIS sub-group was created to carry responsibility for this topic. The first meeting identified two immediate problems: that of documenting the 'state-of-the-art' information on this topic for the sub-group's own benefit; and that of conveying this information, and a sense of its importance, to key colleagues in the Commission of the European Communities, other Community institutions and Member States whose attitudes toward the human dimension of technology would be instrumental in determining the ultimate success of INSIS.

The sub-group decided to combine these objectives by organizing a workshop for our colleagues and using the presentations of top experts as a basis for the definitive book which was lacking. This is that book. It grew out of a series of meetings between the editors and the workshop contributors which took place over a period of almost a year. We had three full-scale co-ordination meetings, numerous smaller meetings on other occasions and countless telephone calls and letters to make the pieces come together. The chapters based on the workshop presentations have been augmented by five additional chapters, whose topics and authors were selected in consultation with the workshop contributors. This is therefore not the usual loosely-edited collection of workshop papers.

Each author approaches the general topic independently. In order to maintain the coherence of these individual perceptions, the editors have allowed a certain amount of overlap between the subject matter covered in some chapters. Overall, however, there is agreement about the key issues and how they should be handled. This consensus reflects a growing awareness, based on the evidence of research into experiences with computer-based services, that the implementation of new office technology will not succeed unless sufficient respect is paid to human and organizational dimensions in the design and development of office information systems.

Harry J. Otway   *Malcolm Peltu*
Besozzo   *London*

CHAPTER 1: THE NATURE OF NEW OFFICE TECHNOLOGY

André Danzin

INTRODUCTION

Many people who work in offices fear the advance of new technology into their work. They are concerned that they will have to adapt suddenly from the equipment of their traditional craft to a world which will look more like an electronics laboratory than an office. The main aim of this book is to examine the likely changes that will take place in the office environment in the future — changes which, it is recommended, should progress at an evolutionary pace rather than attempting to stage an overnight technological coup. This chapter provides an insight into the nature of the technologies which are referred to throughout the book.

Some of the fear of the technology arises because of its apparent mystique and complexity. In describing the technology, this chapter emphasizes the importance of having a 'feeling' for what it can do, rather than wasting effort in trying to understand the inner working of the electronic nervous system of the 'black boxes' which are the engines of the technology. One does not need to know the equations of dynamic balance to ride a bicycle or the thermodynamic principles of the internal combustion engine to drive a motor car. The technical operation of modern equipment should be transparent to the user, whether of a car or a computer-based office system.

INFORMATION AND MACHINES

Office staff spend most of their time on four operations:

— *information capture:* collecting information;

— *information processing:* carrying out tasks on information, such as merging it with other data, performing calculations on it, editing it and so on;

— *information storage:* storing information in files;

— *information retrieval:* accessing the files to find information when needed.

The common factor in all these operations is information, or *data*, as information is also called, particularly in computer-based work. Electronic machines are essentially no more than aids in performing these information handling tasks. They can carry out work at speeds of up to 100 million times faster than people. It is people, however, who should remain in charge of these machines.

What is important is not so much the machine but the information. Whatever aids are used, people working in offices still retain all their responsibilities over the information. In exploring the nature of the new office technologies, the first step is to analyze the nature of information itself.

People do not have a monopoly on information. The higher animals communicate by mimicry and sounds and the basic biological cells carry genetic information. The simplest living organism, the virus, carries as much information as a page of text. Even in a mineral, an atom uses information to communicate with its neighbours to form an organized structure rather than take up random positions. The information that can be handled by minerals is extremely simple, consisting of just two states (called *binary)*. A magnet, for example, knows only north or south, positive or negative. All electronic machines rely on the binary information capability of inert bodies to be able to represent the two states of *digital* information, 1 and 0. This elementary unit could be regarded as a 'grain' of information and is called a *bit* (an abbreviation of *bi*nary dig*it*). The basic elements of a mathematical logic developed in the nineteenth century by George Boole also rely on binary grains, which take the value *true* or *false* and can also be represented as a 1 or 0.

Office technologies using electronics, computing and telecommunications enable information to be collected, processed, transmitted, stored and retrieved in this granular digital form. Text, diagrams, still and moving pictures, speech and other forms of information can be translated into a digital code, in a similar way to which the Morse Code of 'dots' and 'dashes' was used in telegraphy to represent letters of the alphabets and the digits 0 to 9. A computer digital code based on units of seven bits, for example, is able to assign unique combinations of seven 0/1 digits to 128 different *alphanumeric* characters — letters of the alphabet, decimal numerals, punctuation marks and mathematical signs. The principles of Boolean logic provide the mechanism for performing information processing tasks also in digital form.

Binary information granules are therefore fundamental elements in building a unified way of representing and processing information in electronic form.

THE BASIC ELEMENTS OF NEW OFFICE TECHNOLOGIES

There are two main ingredients in information technology, *hardware* and *software*. Hardware is the visible, physical equipment, such as key-boards, screens, printers and electronic components. Software is the 'invisible' set of detailed *program* instructions which automatically controls the hardware.

Electronic components
Electronic components are to computing and information technology what our cells are to our own bodies. They are the elements in which the principal operations are carried out according to an inbuilt program which co-ordinates the way the whole system works. There are various types of these electronic 'cells', each performing a specialized task of logical processing, storage or transmission. Figure 1.1 identifies some of the key technologies used in new office information systems. It shows the dates when they emerged, their struggle for selection and their explosive growth since the 1950s.

The main advances have been achieved in two important technologies:

— *Microelectronics*. In the 1960s, only one active element (a memory bit or a switch used in logical processing, called a *gate*) could be stored on a single sliver of silicon chip; silicon, a constituent of sand, is the most widely used semiconductor material used for transistors. In 1970, over 4,000 elements could be held on an integrated circuit chip. By 1980, *Very Large Scale Integration* (VLSI) had enabled over 60,000 elements to be placed on a chip. In the 1980s, further improvements of tenfold to a hundredfold are likely. The number of failures per unit of time has been reduced by over 10 million-fold since the 1950s.

Telecommunications. Over 100,000 times more information can be sent by telecommunications, with some optical fibres now capable of carrying over 1,000 million bits per second.

These advances have meant that, between 1960 and 1980, there has been a 10,000-fold improvement in such key aspects of information technology hardware as: volume and weight for equal performance; operating speed; price reduction; and energy consumption. Amongst the various technological species in Figure 1.1, particular note should be made of the sub-kingdom of semiconductors which led to the development of microprocessors used to create low cost, small sized and high capability computer-based systems and information storage devices.

The software barrier

The sophisticated tasks that computer-based systems can undertake are dependent on the writing of very long and complicated programs by skilled and highly paid specialists, called *programmers*. The writing of software programs, which could run into many thousands of instructions, has remained closer to scientific craftsmanship, unlike the automated, mass production techniques that could be applied to the development of electronic components. Software development has therefore been less

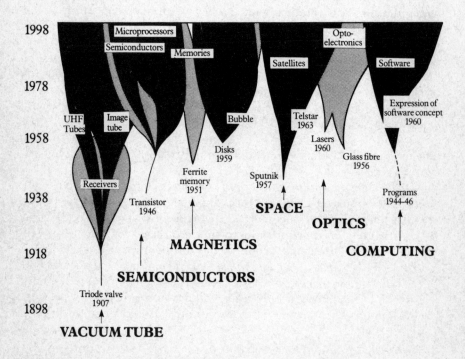

Figure 1.1 Basic elements of information technology (with dates of their emergence)

predictable, less reliable and more costly than hardware production techniques.

In 1955, software represented less than 20 per cent of the total cost of a system. By 1970, the costs were split 50:50. By 1980, software represented well over 80 per cent of the total[1]. This is a real barrier to the rapid spread of applications of all the new products and services comprising new office technologies. Under no circumstances should attempts be made to economize on the skills or cash investment required to develop and support suitable software.

Total systems costs
The total cost of office information systems has not followed the dramatic fall in costs of their electronic components, although there have been significant improvements in total systems cost relative to performance. This is partly because of the growing costs of software, both in absolute terms and as a proportion of total systems costs. In addition, products need to be properly engineered to take account of ergonomic needs (see Chapters 10 and 11).

Responsible vendors and user organizations must invest a great deal of resources to prepare good documentation, provide suitable training, and ensure there is efficient and reliable maintenance and support. These 'hidden extras' are of vital importance to the effective use of computer-based systems and must be carefully evaluated when selecting systems. The cheapest hardware may not be the ideal solution. Manufacturers have also frequently decided to provide customers with increasing capabilities instead of reducing prices.

CONVERGENCE OF COMPUTING, TELECOMMUNICATIONS AND ELECTRONICS

Between 1950 and 1970, important developments in the specialists areas of computing, telecommunications and electronics seemed to be happening in isolation. During the 1970s, however, they converged into what has become known as *information technology* or *telematics*, of which new office technology is a subset. The increases in efficiency caused by this convergence have been vast.

Although computers were first conceived of in the nineteenth century, the major advances occurred in the 1940s and 50s. The key breakthrough was the development of the *general purpose, stored program control* computer.

The main ingredients are shown in Figure 1.2. The software programs and data needed for immediate operation are stored in *main memory* (typically made of semiconductors). Other programs and information are held in *auxiliary* or *backing* storage, typically disks or other magnetic media. The processing unit is also usually made from semiconductor material. Input and output devices are the hardware most visible to the user, such as keyboards, screens and printers.

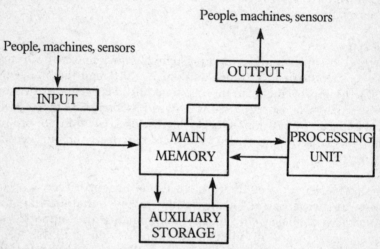

Figure 1.2   Basic elements of a general-purpose, stored program control computer

While computer scientists were developing these principles, telecommunications was advancing, particularly through the use of electronic telephone switch exchanges. Remote communication by voice (the telephone) and the written word (telex) had become commonplace many years before. Meanwhile, the electronics industry was perfecting radio transmission techniques involving no material medium. A wide variety of equipment, such as valves and Cathode Ray Tubes (CRTs), were invented for transforming sensory signals into electronic signals and vice versa. Sounds and images picked up by microphones and cameras could be re-created at the other end on a television set by a CRT and loudspeaker.

The way in which these techniques could converge was shown by the development of what were known as *time sharing, online* or *real-time* computing services. A device, called a *terminal*, can be linked by telephone line to a computer. A typical terminal is a *Visual Display Terminal* (VDT), also called a *Visual Display Unit* (VDU). This consists of a typewriter-style keyboard and associated CRT display. Keying a letter on the keyboard generates the character on the screen. In addition it creates a communications signal which can be regenerated at the other end into a code for computer processing or as characters to be printed. The computer can also generate electronic signals and transmit them back to the terminal under program control, to be displayed on the screen. In this way, the user can have an *interactive* dialogue with the system, for example as used by airline booking clerks to make reservations.

The synthesis of information technologies has led to new office technologies such as enhanced telephones, keyboards for computer data and program input, VDTs, centralized and free-standing local computers, printers, computer storage, sophisticated reprographic equipment, voice synthesizers and graph plotters. As has been explained, the key to these systems is the digitalization of information into their 'granular' 0/1 bits. Once information has been translated into these elementary units, they can be blended under software control to reconstruct any kind of message and to enable information processing, retrieval or look-up to be carried out efficiently, irrespective of the distance involved. This is possible because costs have fallen, transmission can be effected at the speed of light, and there is a high degree of reliability.

The widely used prefix 'tele' signifies that many office functions with which we are already familiar in a local context can be carried out remotely, as if distance itself no longer existed.

THE MAIN NEW OFFICE TECHNOLOGIES

This background is sufficient to show the underlying concepts and techniques that are applicable to office work. Now we can look at the equipment and systems being introduced to offices, paying special attention to what they do rather than how they do it. The main problem in describing the technologies is the speed at which they are developing. A family photograph is difficult to take if everybody is running about. The subject of office technology is similarly turbulent. The classification of new technology in Figure 1.3 is according to my personal order of priority in terms of the underlying impact on working conditions.

Classification	*Examples*
Direct aids to efficiency	— enhanced telephony — word processors — electronic filing — personal computing
Improved communications systems	— local data network — message handling facility — telecopying — teleconferencing — multifunction workstation
Decision-making aids	— databases — modelling systems — *expert* systems

Figure 1.3: Types of new office technologies

DIRECT AIDS TO OFFICE EFFICIENCY

Equipment is available which can improve efficiency in the carrying out of traditional office tasks. In themselves, they are unlikely to make fundamental changes in working conditions or human ways of thinking but they can be remarkably effective instruments when implemented in the appropriate manner.

Telephone aids
The ordinary telephone can be transformed by the addition of semiconductor memory and processing, displays, computerbased telephone exchanges and other information technologies. Such an *enhanced telephony* device could, for example, retain in its memory the telephone numbers for frequently dialled calls. By keying-in a brief code, the required number would be automatically called; if it is engaged, it would be redialled. The number and name of the persons being called would be displayed on the associated screen.

A built-in memory in the enhanced telephone could be used to record incoming messages and act like a telephone answering machine when the caller is out. A programming capability could enable the telephone device to be instructed by the user to carry out various tasks automatically, for example re-routing calls to another number if the user is in a different office temporarily or making a call to a particular number at a predetermined time. The enhanced telephone can resemble a computer terminal and could perform tasks like accessing databases, 'reading' a document automatically then relaying the contents over a telephone line using a synthesized voice. Continuous displaying of the cost of a call, encryption and deciphering of information during transmission to maintain absolute security and many other facilities become available when the telephone plus micro-processor plus memory plus video display are combined with the human imagination.

Word processing
A word processor is a machine with a keyboard similar to a familiar typewriter keyboard (see Figure 1.4). In addition, it usually has a screen to display the typed text, a memory unit and letter-quality printer, all controlled by a computer processor with appropriate software. The screen can vary in length from a single line to a full page display. On a basic *electronic typewriter,* which has a single-line display, the available memory may just be a few words or lines. On larger, more sophisticated word processors, the storage is typically on a magnetic medium. In early

Figure 1.4   Typists at typical word processors with keyboards and associated screens; a letter-quality printer is to the left of the typist in the foreground

machines, the magnetic card was popular but these have been replaced by *floppy disks* or *diskettes*. These look like flexible 45 rpm records and can store about a hundred pages of A4 text on a single disk. *Hard disks* available with bigger systems can store many thousands of pages of text.

The word processor's keyboard and screen is equivalent to the input and output mechanisms of a VDT or a small general purpose computer. With suitable software, general purpose computers can be used for word processing tasks. The term 'word processor' is applied to equipment designed specifically for text handling office tasks.

The significant advance of word processors compared to traditional typewriters is their ability to automatically *edit* text. As information is keyed-in, it is stored in digital coded form in memory. Words, sentences and other segments of text can then be deleted, added, changed and moved around under software control, without affecting unaltered text. This avoids the necessity to rewrite and check complete drafts of memos, letters, reports and other documents. If standard text is used for most of a document that requires just a few variations, such as name, address and other details specific to the recipient of the document, the word processor can store the unchanging text. When linked to files containing the variable information, a number of different documents can be typed automatically, with each one tailor-made to the individual recipient.

Word processing devices can be interlinked in networks to provide, for example, the *teletex* capability, which is like a 'super telex' and is compatible with the telex network. This is a form of *electronic mail*. The term 'teletex' includes the service, the equipment and the standards for the remote exchange of texts with the optimum security and speed.

Electronic filing

Instead of filing information in its paper *(hard copy)* form, electronic systems can store it using magnetic (such as disks and tapes) or optical techniques (such as laser-based *video disks*). The saving in space is considerable. The contents of a complete filing cabinet could be reduced to a hard disk of less volume than a single cabinet drawer or even to one video disk. The time to access and retrieve information can be reduced to a few seconds and stored information can be printed out in hard copy form whenever required.

The effectiveness of such filing systems depends on the availability of suitable software and computer processing capabilities. Such specialist software can be complex to develop and should give high priority to the human requirement of being able to learn and use the system easily.

Personal computing

General computing capabilities designed for use by an individual or small group are known as *personal computing*. Typically, this is a self-contained *microcomputer* or *desk-top computer* with keyboard, screen, processing, storage and printed output capability. Some microcomputers are small enough to be carried around in a briefcase-style holder. A microcomputer can be linked into a telecommunications network via a coupling unit. This could be done through the public telephone network, giving microcomputer users connections to other users and access to a variety of sources of computerized information and processing.

Personal computing capabilities could also be offered on VDTs which are part of a wider computing network. A personal computing facility should provide the range of functions expected on large systems, although the size and extent of the problems that can be solved would be smaller than for larger systems. Typical personal computing capabilities include the handling of accounts; automatically comparing actual financial and trading results with planned budgets; aids to strategic decision making; keeping an *electronic diary* for arranging meetings and automatically prompting the user of important forthcoming events; and transforming numerical tables into graphs and charts.

In addition to being used in the office, microcomputers can be operated at home or while travelling. Programs can be developed unique to their owners and controls incorporated to ensure that their information can remain confidential. A typical microcomputer looks similar to the word processor in Figure 1.4, although with a keyboard designed for general data processing tasks and, often, an ordinary television set as a screen.

MEANS OF COMMUNICATION

A number of new means of communicating within offices and to outside locations are being made available by information technology. They are not simply aids to productivity but will probably result in behavioural changes in person-to-person communications. These new techniques will affect every level and type of staff within an organization and will need to be learnt by all office personnel.

Local data networks

The convergence of information technologies makes it necessary to enable a variety of digital information capabilities to be integrated within the same service — not just voice and text messages but also computer data and images (still or moving). A considerable amount of information communication takes place within an organization. *Local Area Networks* (LANs) have therefore been developed to enable large volumes of information to be transmitted within relatively short distances; networks providing links over longer distances are sometimes called *Wide Area Networks* (WANs). A LAN typically has a range of a few kilometres and a capacity of several millions of bits per second. Such a network can connect a variety of office information systems and devices from different manufacturers. Each unit linked to the network is known as a *workstation* or, simply, as a *station*. Word processors, electronic filing systems, microcomputers, small business systems *(minicomputers),* large central *mainframe* computers and even equipment in production centres could be stations on a local network.

Figure 1.5 illustrates the general plan for a local network. The interface is necessary, just as a plug-and-socket is needed to connect electrical devices to an electricity grid. Protocols are the procedures,

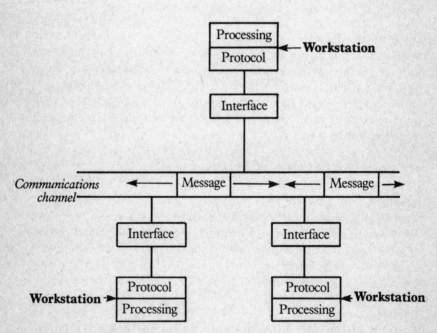

Figure 1.5   General plan of a Local Area Network

standards and rules which govern the way information is exchanged within the network and which must enable different types of devices to be integrated into the same service.

LAN techniques vary both in terms of the type of communications link (coaxial cables or fibre optic cables) and in the structure and access methods used. Three of the most widely used forms are *broadcast, ring* and *star* structures. With a broadcast system, such as *Ethernet* developed by Xerox Corporation, messages are transmitted into communications, channels as soon as they are ready, with stations picking up their messages in an equivalent way to which a radio receiver tunes into broadcast signals. A ring system has stations linked on a circular connection, around which a continuous 'belt' of data units are sent and picked up, as if the ring had a number of buckets circulating around it, into which items can be loaded and off-loaded. A star network gets its name because all stations are linked to a single focus, like rays from a star's nucleus. A computer-based *Private Automatic Branch Exchange* (PABX), similar to telephone exchanges, is a typical switch device in a star network.

Electronic mail and message handling
Electronic mail includes all equipment and services for document transmission, such as telex, teletex and telecopying. Some of these have been available for many years using *analogue* techniques. Analogue methods were used before the development of digital techniques, particularly in telephone and telex networks. Analogue transmission is made by reproducing the form of a physical signal. Digital transmission is superior in terms of efficiency, reliability and quality, so is replacing analogue communications.

Message handling systems add a computer-based system to store and manage messages to basic electronic mail capabilities. In such a system, messages can be held in computer memory which acts as an *electronic mailbox*. Stored messages can subsequently be forwarded to the recipient when requested. The technique is therefore called *store-and-forward* systems. This means that messages can be sent when convenient to the sender, and picked up when convenient to the recipient, thus avoiding a great deal of wasted effort and time in trying to contact a person directly.

The message handling facility allows the same message to be routed to many correspondents. It also assists in handling the protocols needed to establish compatibility between different terminals. The switching is carried out automatically using lists of correspondents, calling charges, and so on. The message is usually received and displayed on a VDT screen. A printer can be used if it is necessary to have a hard copy of the message to keep. Messages can be stored for however long is needed.

Telecopying

Network transmission techniques, called *telecopying* or *facsimile* (fax), provide a remote version of the photocopying reproduction services already so familiar and so indispensable.The user at one end of the line places a piece of paper in the fax transceiver (see Figure 1.6). A

Figure 1.6   A facsimile device showing a document being fed into the unit; a copy of it will be made on a similar device at the other end of a link made by dialling a number with an ordinary telephone handset

copy of the document is then produced at a similar device at the receiving end of the transmission link.

Teleconferencing

The need to consult others, to communicate one's reactions, to explain and to arrive at a consensus increases with the complexity of an organization's management and its administrative operations. Teleconferencing can be a useful and efficient means of having meetings which avoids the need for individuals to travel and helps reduce the resultant costs and loss of time.

An *audio* or *audiographic conference* is limited to the exchange of sounds, graphics and text, using the combined resources of multiple interconnected telephones, telecopying and *telewriting* (transmitting handwriting and drawings). To these, the *video conference* adds display screens, such as television sets, or *videophones (viewphones)*. In computer-based conferencing, the store-and-forward message handling facilities are employed to enable participants to exchange messages from terminals.

Teleconferencing can require the use of specially-equipped rooms. Ideally, there should be no more than four or five participants at each centre, with no more than three or four centres in the conference. Contributions can be effective, provided those taking part are properly prepared, and brief and to the point in their contributions.

Multifunction and executive workstations

Some workstations allow a variety of different capabilities to be carried out from the same device, such as text keyboarding, displays, voice input, and electronic mail. These *multifunction* workstations could be used by managers, professionals and secretaries, whose main task is more than just typing. Special *executive workstations* have been developed, tailored to the kinds of communications, calculations and decision-making activities that characterize the work of managers and senior administrators.

EQUIPMENT FOR A NEW GENERATION OF OFFICE WORK

So far I have considered only those technologies and equipment which relate to relatively simple efficiency requirements or new communications methods. With databases, decision-making aids and 'expert' systems, we enter a domain of techniques likely to have a more profound effect on patterns of thought and action.

Databases and videotex

Computer storage can be used to hold vast *databanks*, collections of information relating to a specific area of knowledge [2]. With appropriate software, these can be developed into *databases* which are managed so that users can search, retrieve, update, summarise, calculate and perform other actions on the information stored in it. This *DataBase Management Systems* (DBMS) software also ensures the integrity, confidentiality and security of the information.

Databases may be purely internal within an organization or they may be computerized libraries made available through 'hosts' — organizations that operate computers to allow subscribers to their service to consult their databases, often concentrating on areas of special scientific or professional interest. The input of vast quantities of data, its verification, standardization and coding require continuous, tricky and expensive work. Any organization entering into database systems, whether for internal use or as a host, must therefore be willing to invest considerable resources on an ongoing basis.

Videotex (also known as *viewdata*) is a particular version of a database service. Information in a viewdata system is organized into 'pages', similar to the structure of a magazine. Public videotex services are provided by many national telecommunications authorities; some organizations or groups of organizations have developed their own private videotex services. *Broadcast videotex (teletext)* provides a one-way flow of data pages from a source such as a television transmitter which can be interpreted by a specially adapted television set.

The nature of languages used to make enquiries of database systems is discussed by Sigurd Jensen in Chapter 11.

Models that aid decision-making

Software can be developed to provide *simulation models* which reproduce the physical, economic or financial procedures which link data to the variations the user wishes to study. Simulations can be made of the flight of an aircraft, the budget of a business or the economy of a country. These models are based on the principle of *causality*. If the input data is changed, an 'effect' will be caused and the program will be able to calculate it. If various scenarios are considered by inputting different information *variables*, the different results forecast by the models can aid decision making by providing guidance on strategic choices.

Such methods, known as *Decision Support Systems*, will be used increasingly for complex decisions, for example in international negotiations concerning quotas and tariffs or in taking business decisions in a volatile economic environment. Such modelling methods, however, are not perfect. They are biased according to the way the program has been prepared. They also simplify reality, which can never be fully catalogued or turned into the 'straight-line' logic needed by computers.

Software models can only predict the kinds of outcome foreseen by their designers. They cannot cope with situations inconsistent with the basic assumptions. This type of decision-making aid does, however, have three particular advantages:

— It compels the user to define the 'laws' which govern phenomena. This sometimes exposes remarkable gaps in knowledge.

— It encourages people to co-operate and work together, provided it is accepted that the construction of the model and its results should be the subject of discussion.

— Work on the model has considerable educational value.

Expert systems
If, as the Japanese government has done [3], we consider the needs of the twenty first century, database and decision making aids need to be complemented by what are called *expert systems*. These have the ability to learn and to reason, in an analogous way to a human expert. They were first used for physical and biological systems, for example, diagnosing the cause of breakdowns in complex machines or assisting in medical diagnoses. Expert systems can also be applied to many areas of government, business and industry to provide advice of the same quality as specialist human 'consultants'. Expert systems open up the potential for imaginative ways of applying scientific method to economic, social and political problems.

STAFF PREPARATION

The remainder of this book examines in detail how to introduce new office technologies in ways which are acceptable to the individual and social requirements of people working in offices. A computer-based system inflicted without any preparation of staff will be rejected and it will take several years to overcome the effects of this traumatic experience. The main elements of this preparation should be *gradual change* and *training*.

The technology may have made progress at a revolutionary pace since the 1950s but new systems should be introduced item by item, without submerging staff under an unreasonable flood of difficult new procedures all at once. Training must be provided systematically to all staff who will come into contact with new technology — and that is likely to mean virtually everyone working in an office. Training needs could vary from a few days or weeks to learn how to operate word processing or electronic filing systems, to a continuing long-term process for managers coping with complex technical, organizational, human and technical changes.

New office informatology will eventually force us to rethink all our systems of interpersonal relationships and other aspects of office work. The 'information renaissance' is a great adventure and a great challenge.

RECOMMENDATIONS

1 Do not place undue stress on the technological *means* (the equipment and technology) at the expense of the *ends* (making good use of information) of new office systems.

2 Do not needlessly try to know all the details of the technology. A general 'feel' for the principles of digital information representation and software-controlled processing is sufficient background needed to understand the technologies discussed in this chapter.

3 Do not be put off using new office technology because of a fear of not understanding how it works.

4 Do not become a slave of perfection and continually want to move on to new and more advanced systems. Stick to a consistent strategy and avoid constantly changing policy on equipment and software.

REFERENCES

[1] *Datamation*, New York (May 1973).

[2] *Journal Officiel de la République Francaise* (17 January 1982).

[3] Moto-Oka T., *Fifth Generation Computer Systems*, North-Holland Publishing Company, Amsterdam and Elsevier Science Publishing Company, New York (1982).

CHAPTER 2: EVALUATING THE REAL BENEFITS

Anthony G. Hopwood

INTRODUCTION

Computer-based information systems can have pervasive effects on organizational life, including many which do not enter into the original justification of the system. They not only have the potential to alter the nature of work, employment levels, cost structures and the efficiency of operations directly, but can also have major indirect impacts on the whole functioning and performance of the organization over a long period of time.

The remainder of this book examines in detail the consequences of information-system changes for individuals and organizations. This chapter uses many practical examples to provide an overview of key problem areas that have been encountered during such changes. It illustrates the narrow scope and short time focus that often characterizes evaluations of information systems, and suggests a basis for making wider, more strategic assessments that take into account the political nature of the decision-making processes involved.

THE ROLE OF INFORMATION IN ORGANIZATIONAL LIFE

The evaluation of computer-based information systems is a complex endeavour because information plays a key role in most activities in modern organizations. Information is gathered and analyzed to make decisions at all levels. Information delineates organizational structures, the responsibilities of particular units, the nature of managerial authority and associated spheres of discretion and influence. Flows of information disseminate organizational goals and missions, forge the linkages between organizational units and assist the co-ordination and integration of the complicated interactions between specialized tasks.

Information therefore creates perceptions of organizational reality and is

actively involved in supporting and effecting work activities. It is
neither a static nor a self-contained phenomenon but permeates all
functions. A new information system can influence and sometimes
radically alter the environments that need to be managed. Yet many
computer-based information systems are introduced on the basis of
limited administrative, economic and technical analyses and
expectations.

Organizational flexibility

An information system can hinder or help an organization's ability to
adapt to meet new challenges. For example[1], after introducing the
extensive use of automated control processes and robotics, a large motor
manufacturer realized that it had successfully automated the traditional
concept of an assembly line, building in all the rigidities of the old process.
About the same time, a key competitor had introduced new systems only
after a more fundamental evaluation of the potential of information
technologies which questioned the need to maintain the previous
manufacturing rigidities. The competitor's resultant system was much
more flexible, even though it employed similar technological components. This flexibility gave the competitor considerable strategic and
economic advantage when the automobile market became volatile and
unpredictable.

Similarly, an insurance company planned to introduce a new type of
policy. To promote it, the company wanted to identify all of their existing
policy-holders, between certain ages, who did not have the relevant cover.
This is an ideal task for an integrated computerized database management system but the relevant information within the company was on
different files. While these files were being integrated, at great expense
and with difficulty, a competitor launched a similar policy. 'We lost out
because our information systems had just about set like concrete,'
commented the Managing Director.

Organizational control

Information systems reinforce or change relationships between central
authorities and local departments and agents. A manufacturing company operating through subsidiaries around the world, for example,
reinforced centralized control by introducing a global computerized
system which gave direct, updated reports on cash and fund flows directly
to corporate headquarters. This provided a mechanism to implement
effectively the management policy of having each subsidiary responsible
for generating profits against an annual plan and contributing to an
annual dividend in cash to corporate funds.

On the other hand, a government department used an information system to devolve management control, by introducing new office technology to facilitate the collection of information in its geographically remote regions. This enabled regional managers to have more direct control over local costs. It also implied a passing of authority to the regions to initiate actions which previously required central sanction. This led to a backlash from some officers at the centre who felt their authority and status had been eroded.

Indirect impacts

The implications of a new information system often extend into areas outside the context for which they were initially introduced. For example, a central information system implemented by a credit card company changed the company's marketing strategy. Previously, advertising had to be selective and upmarket as a means of controlling who was allowed to use its card. However, the new information system could provide up-to-date monitoring of the transactions made by card holders as a means of management control. The advertising policy could therefore be changed to be less selective.

Labour relations are often brought into the development and operation of new information systems (see Chapter 9). For example, when a retail chain installed new 'point of sale' equipment at checkouts, the union asked for the operators' jobs to be upgraded because they were now responsible for providing input into corporate systems. In a British company, the union asked for access to personnel records, which they were entitled to under collective bargaining legislation. From this, the union could tell the labour rates at various plants, which influenced its bargaining position.

A computer-based system can change job functions, which makes a significant difference to an individual's motivation and job satisfaction (see Chapters 8 and 11). For example, when a bank computerized its local branch operations, the main aim was to automate the cashier's work. It also altered the manager's function by shifting much of the accounting and control of branch operations to the head office. As a result, many managers complained that they had become merely 'salesmen' selling central services rather than influential figures in the local business community.

MISTAKES IN EVALUATING COMPUTER-BASED INFORMATION SYSTEMS

Computer-based information technology has the potential to improve many processes involved in managing information. In practice, however, many problems have been encountered in trying to fulfil that potential. The techniques which have traditionally been used to set objectives have tended to look at mainly technical and short-term quantifiable economic criteria. This has been satisfactory for identifying the technical problems that arise from the rapid rate of innovation, but it is inadequate as a means of pinpointing and managing the broader — and crucial — human and organizational aspects.

Despite the massive growth in routine information provision by computer-based systems, many organizations have found that demands for information are still unmet, particularly when faced with newly turbulent environments. Systems based on formal organizational procedures (see Chapter 6) reflect the problems and crises of the past rather than the present 'need-to-know'; unfortunately, such formal systems are the bases for many computer-based information services.

Different evaluation strategies are needed to relate new office technology developments to the whole spectrum of real-world requirements. It must remain important to consider technical, administrative and quantifiable economic elements which have been emphasized in the past. The relationships which information flows have to other aspects of organizational functioning suggest, however, that consideration of these factors is insufficient to comprehend the complexities of the information problems of today's organizations. The main mistakes that have been made in setting objectives and evaluating implementations have been:

— Placing the primary emphasis on short-term economic consequences;

— Evaluating the information system in isolation from organizational functions which they serve — often ignoring human and social consequences or, when they are considered, placing an overemphasis on individualistic needs and physical ergonomics;

— Failing to relate economic and social perspectives;

— Recognizing uncertainties in the future but not giving sufficient priority to providing flexibility in the system to adapt to changes;

—Viewing information in a partial way;

—Taking a limited view of the roles served by information systems in organizations.

The following sections examine the experiences which have brought these problems to light.

Too much short-term economics

When considering investments in new information systems, there is a tendency, as in other investment decisions, to emphasize the relationship between the initial capital costs of the project and the net operating savings. Instead of giving high priority to *value-added* aims, the ways in which the new system can add value to various organizational activities, a dominant position is given to the *cost-substitution* assessment. This calculates savings in personnel costs and financial gains from improved operational activities, such as more efficient inventory control and speedier decisions. The savings are compared to the costs of the new system's capital, operational and development expenditure and related personnel training. In most cases, the primary problems confronted are of a technical and forecasting nature. The image of the change process created by this concentration on short-term economics invariably requires that little consideration is given to other closely related aspects of organizational functioning and to longer-term economic aspects. Attention is focused on those economic factors which can be identified at the time the decision is taken to introduce a new system. This in itself is a complex process and has sometimes missed important practical considerations, such as the support and maintenance costs for the equipment.

Even when care has been taken to try and look deeper than straight cost-substitution analysis, mistakes have been made. A leading European car manufacturer, for example, introduced a vehicle inventory recording system throughout its network of main dealers, enabling each dealer as well as the company to know the location of all stock via immediate direct computing access to the data. A thorough economic appraisal of the system seemed to demonstrate that it could be cost effective, assisting dealers' sales efforts and giving more efficient management of the manufacturer's inventories. Unfortunately, the major economic consequence of the system was not anticipated: the ease of access to inventory information inadvertently induced dealers to reduce their own stocks. Why keep large stocks of cars, they asked, when they could satisfy customers' needs by finding the nearest location of a suitable model at the press of a button? This meant that the manufacturer had to increase its own stocks, which significantly added to its costs.

Another manufacturing company was faced with a sudden increase in competitive pressures. It ordered a complete review of its information systems strategies after finding that the information produced by the computer was mainly oriented towards internal, short-term problems whereas the company's real problems were external and long-term.

Isolating the information system
The calculation and acceptance of short-term economic criteria are simplified if the information system is regarded as a self-contained entity. Growing technological complexities and the increasing influence of technical professionals has meant that such false simplifications have often caused the information function to become isolated from other organizational activities. Lip-service may be paid to concepts like 'information as a corporate resource' but, in practice, information systems can become an almost autonomous development.

The characteristics of the information itself and the information system are emphasized rather than the consequences that these might have. What is needed is a more detailed charting of the specific implications for key activities such as marketing strategies, production options, labour relations and financial structures. In the next chapter, Peter Keen recommends a strategy to handle new office technology products which effectively integrates all aspects.

An example of what can go wrong is the experience of a large oil company which had a sophisticated long-range plan for computer developments. Unfortunately, the strategy had been created separately from product and market development plans and was not updated in phase with changes in the business environment. Eventually, a crisis occurred when there was a fundamental shift in marketing policy. 'We are tending to revert to manual systems to meet the urgent, rapid changes in data needs,' the Chief Executive commented ruefully.

The inward-looking nature of many information systems institutionalize internal management processes and perceptions at a time when increasingly interdependent and volatile world economic, industrial and technological activities mean that more problems come from external sources. The Marketing Director of a major European consumer electronics firm, for example, succeeded in initiating a major review of corporate information system after discovering that it could not cope adequately with changes in the life cycles of products. The average product life cycle had been cut from 7 to 8 years to 1.5 to 2 years. A major management problem was therefore to develop strategies which would span across life cycles but the information system was optimized to handle within-life-cycle performance.

Inadequate attention to human and social consequences
During the first phase of commercial computing in the 1960s and early 1970s, hardly any attention was given to the human and social consequences of computing. Most users of the systems were given special training to handle generally complex and difficult-to-use systems. When microelectronics caused computing to come closer to real working environments, such as the office, increasing attention was paid to the individual's use of systems (see Chapters 10 and 11).

Research was carried out, particularly into the physical ergonomic design of systems to make them safe, comfortable and easy to use. The nature of the software interaction between user and system and the impact of the system on individuals' motivation and productivity also began to be regarded by managers as a significant factor in information system changes. This concern was sharpened by laws on ergonomics introduced in some West European countries and by pressure from trade unions (see Chapter 9). The interest in these aspects was a step in the right direction but its partial nature should be noted. The emphasis has been individualistic rather than on the broader organizational ramifications.

The emphasis on individualistic and ergonomic aspects can be made compatible with the narrow short-term economic and technical perspectives discussed above. The advocates of ergonomics usually regard themselves as being in a more 'human' tradition than the rationalist school of 'scientific management' which dominated production-line automation (see Enid Mumford's comparison of Taylorism and socio-technical techniques in Chapter 4). Somewhat paradoxically, however, quantifiable ergonomic standards have often been used by management to reinforce a scientific management approach that would be opposed by many who are sympathetic to the ergonomic approach.

Failing to relate social and economic perspectives
Given that social issues themselves have generally been treated in a partial and haphazard way, it is not surprising that it has been rare for social and economic evaluations to be related. It has also been rare for a social analysis to be used as a way of determining the nature of the economic goals or for economics to be used explicitly to constrain the

assessment of the social environment. Prevailing practices have maintained the autonomy of these two aspects despite the fact that repeated evaluations of information system changes illustrate the limitation of doing this.

The kind of problems which result from this separation were highlighted by the experience of a major North American manufacturing company. It invested in a massive centralized computer-based information service to support key decisions and facilitate planning and scheduling of marketing and production. The same information, however, was also used to set targets to motivate managers. Being aware of its evaluative uses, the managers biased many of the key information flows. The resultant optimistic forecasts led to increased expenditures on unnecessarily high inventories and production line work-in-progress and made for a lack of flexibility in co-ordinating marketing and production activities.

Inability to adapt to the future
When evaluating the consequences of information systems attention is usually given to the improvement of forecasting methods, probabilistic assessments and other techniques which try to decipher future uncertainties. It is less common for recognition and priority to be given to the more fundamental, unpredictable discontinuities which characterize the future. Despite a theoretical genuflection towards the need for information systems to respond to the unexpected, in practice emphasis has usually been placed on the need to identify the most efficient way of responding to what is perceived as a known future.

As the quotation from the Managing Director of the insurance company indicated, the result is that many systems have been 'set in concrete'. Little attention has been given to creating systems which are flexible, responsive and adaptive. In addition to the earlier examples given of the inflexibility of some computer-based systems, an evaluation exercise by an important manufacturing company highlights the far-reaching negative impact of an over-shortsighted design. The company found that its information system had detracted from, rather than enhanced, its operational flexibility, management processes had been made more complex and time consuming, investment in rapid access to *ad-hoc* information had been neglected and management defensiveness had increased.

Over-emphasizing formal information flows
There has been a tendency to stress the official routine flows of information when designing computer-based systems, despite the fact

that many studies of the way organizations work stress the significance of the diversity of other information channels[2]. A summary of the main type of information flows is given in Figure 2.1. Computer-based systems have provided an explosion of 'official-routine' information in activities such as personnel, materials management, inventory control, production control and many other management and administrative functions. This is supplemented by unofficial but still routine information kept in 'black books' or 'in the desk drawer', which individuals feel they need to make decisions. 'Just-in-case' files contain routine but unofficial information, which an individual feels could be used in defence of decisions and actions.

	Routine	Non-routine
Official	Computer-based information systems	*Ad hoc* queries Direct access to data Task forces
Unofficial	Black books Just-in-case files	The 'grapevine' Lunch-table chats

Figures 2.1. Types of information flow

Informal information flows play an important role in all organizations. These are passed via the grapevines and *ad hoc* chats which permeate managerial, office and shop floor circles and are facilitated by close personal proximity or by membership of clubs and outside organizations. Even official computer-based systems can be used to provide non-routine *ad hoc* enquiries or to give direct access to a database. Structural changes are also made in the organization, such as the setting up of task forces to improve communications channels.

Computer-based systems are primarily used in — and emphasize — official information routines, although the unofficial, alternative information flows are known to play strategic roles in organizational activities. These important unofficial communications can be endangered unless the partial role played by official information is recognized and active steps taken to understand and cater for the complex informal sources of information which contribute to organizational performance.

The dangers of failing to investigate the organizational impact of un-official information was dramatically illustrated by the experiences of a

British company. It had emerged as the only large company in its sector to survive a turbulent period, although it was in a lean and financially insecure state. Management initiated rationalizations, including the dispersal of two-thirds of head office staff to a suburban site, and expansion of the existing computer-based system to provide 'better information on management efficiency'. Shortly before implementing these plans, a consultant undertook a survey of information flows, which led to the abandonment of the move. The consultant found that the company had survived the crisis that had hit the industry primarily because of the close physical proximity of key organizational members. This enabled messages from the volatile outside world to be transmitted through the company and acted on very quickly. That role had not been recognized in the original plan.

Another example of the problems with partial information occurred in a hospital which intended to introduce new office technology. One aim was to 'rationalize' the information flows, which had been shown to include a substantial amount of 'redundant' information which was either dupli-cated or unused. Instead of producing the expected cost savings, the change was a painful process, with many key organizational processes grinding to a halt. The reason was that no consideration had been given to the important role of the 'redundant' information in assisting staff motivation and the co-ordination of activities. Although it did not help senior management to monitor lower level performance, it did help local managers to understand what was going on in their own areas. Eventually that so-called redundant information had to be provided again, at a higher cost than with the original system.

Ignoring the political role of information
Most evaluations of computer-based information systems give primacy to the 'rational' role which such systems are deemed to service, such as 'facilitating decision making, providing 'quicker, more accurate and relevant' information or assisting in the 'efficient' allocation of resources. Participants in the organization, however, realize that this is a limited view of the real role of information.

Information system requirements are closely related to organizational power and emerge from essentially political processes which characterize organizational life[4]. Although official evaluations attempt to suggest that new systems are neutral technical artifacts, there is strong grassroots awareness that this 'rational' perception is a very partial representation of reality. Based on the work of two American sociologists, Michael Earl and I have categorized the different roles that the same information system can take within an organization (see Figure 2.2)[3]. The important elements, which they believe determine the role of the information system, are the degree of certainty/uncertainty that applies to the objectives of actions and to the cause and effect relationships underlying organizational processes.

| | | Objectives | |
		Certain	Uncertain
Cause and effect relationships	Certain	Answer Machine	Ammunition Machine
	Uncertain	Learning Machine	Rationalization Machine

Figure 2.2. Various roles of information systems

When the cause and effect and objectives are both certain, decisions tend to be made in a computational manner, using the information system as a mechanistic 'answer machine', within a highly structured and well understood decision-making process. With increasing uncertainty of the cause and effect relationship, the information system can assist the decision-maker to exercise subjective judgements. It acts as a 'learning machine', which helps the user to understand the context in which he or she is operating and to find out about some of the uncertainties involved.

Where there is uncertainty about objectives but the underlying cause and effects of decisions are certain, demands for information arise from the process of managing an environment characterized by conflict and bargaining. Information systems in this context serve as 'ammunition machines' used to support a particular case or to shape a picture of 'reality'. If all certainty disappears, 'inspirational' decision-making has to be used. In this case, information is marshalled by a retrospective 'rationalization machine' to legitimate actions already taken.

The roles of information systems as answering or learning machines are the main substance of official computer system designs and evaluations. Information specialists are reluctant to be associated with the more 'political' roles because it is threatening to them. They like to use the traditional and partial approaches criticized earlier in this chapter to provide partial and short-term ammunition and rationalizations to defend their supposedly neutral technology.

EVALUATION AS A SOCIAL PROCESS

This chapter has illustrated some of the mistakes in making narrow and shortsighted evaluations of computer-based information systems. It is possible, however, to extend the horizons of economic assessments to include, at least in qualitative form, organizational considerations of a more strategic nature. The remainder of this book examines methods of implementing such broader perspectives, in particular by explicitly integrating human, organizational and social consequences with technical and economic considerations.

Such techniques, however, will merely serve to provide better and more refined 'answer' and 'learning machines' unless there is a recognition of the political context in which the information system has a key role. Evaluations should take into account the political interests of various groups with different interests and concerns. This would sharpen the perceptions of problems, influence the options available for action and assist in adapting the resultant system to real requirements. There is no magic formula, however, which can solve what is intrinsically a complex and unpredictable task. As Rob Kling analyzes in Chapter 13, information system planning and design must satisfy pluralistic and often conflicting demands. Issues that need to be decided range far beyond purely technical considerations or factors which can be simplified in terms of isolated applications of the technology. Typical questions that arise include: Should decision processes be centralized or decentralized? Will changes create more or less social interaction? Will organizational flexibility be lost or will information systems enable the organization to cope more effectively with a volatile environment? Does the system increase the efficiency of social surveillance and control? Can computer-based systems replicate the subtle, informal, personal communications on which all organizations depend? How can society in general cope with the employment and training implications of information technology?

Technical and short-term economic aspects cannot be separated from the social dimensions of these impacts. The only way to resolve questions such as these is explicitly to recognize the political aspects of decision making. One way of doing this has been for some interest groups to press for legislation and to negotiate agreements which provide staff with rights to participate in taking decisions which influence the direction of technological change. Generally, however, the technically-oriented approach has predominated because it is based on relatively well-developed methodologies (although there are many difficult unsolved technical problems) and tends to reinforce the existing and well established power structures.

Both the technical and political perspectives of new office technology require a great deal of live practical experience before they can provide a mature understanding of exactly how to manage the total process of technological change to take account of the multiplicity of interactions and implications. A first step in that direction is at least to recognize that evaluations of information systems should face up to the whole spectrum of human and organizational aspects which has been highlighted in this chapter and is further examined in the rest of the book.

RECOMMENDATIONS

1 Acknowledge that the setting of goals and evaluation of information systems is a political process involving many groups and individuals with vested interests.

2 Seek to illuminate the various interests and their consequence for the eventual evaluation process.

3 Examine the mechanisms for the representation of different interests, the institutional means by which divergent evaluations can be discussed and the ability of different groups to have access to informed opinion and relevant data regarding the options available.

4 Recognize that evaluations can take place from different perspectives — the individual, the group, the organization and the social.

5 Give active consideration to the ways in which new information systems will influence the diversity of official and unofficial information flows.

6 Never evaluate an information system in isolation from its organizational context and consider the ramifications of information system developments for the operation, performance and integration of various functions in the organization.

7 Consider the importance of ensuring that the information system is

flexible and adaptive, particularly in a world characterized by uncertainty and the occurrence of the unexpected.

8 Avoid evaluations that divorce social aspects from economic factors.

9 Question the apparent certainties of short-term evaluative exercises and probe the assumptions of simple, short-term cost-benefit justifications of new systems.

10 Be aware that the evaluation exercise is itself a complex information processing activity, subject to all the problems and opportunities which characterize this area.

REFERENCES

1 Examples in this chapter are taken from a number of sources, including Tricker, R.I., *Effective Information Management*, Beaumont Executive Press, Oxford, UK, 1982.

2 Minzberg, H., *How Managers Manage*, Harper & Row, New York, 1974.

3 Earl, M., Hopwood, A.G., 'From Management Information to Information Management' in Lucas, H.F. *et al* (eds) *'The Information System Environment*, North-Holland, Amsterdam, 1980.

4 Burchell, S., Clubb, C., Hopwood, A.G., Hughes, J., Nahapet, J., 'The Role of Accounting in Organizations and Society', *Accounting, Organizations and Society*, Vol 5, No 2, 1980.

CHAPTER 3: STRATEGIC PLANNING FOR THE NEW SYSTEM

Peter G.W. Keen

INTRODUCTION

The distinguishing feature of new office technology is not its technical building blocks but the aggressive nature of its implementors' mission: to establish information technology as a central contributor to 'productivity' and a component of all secretarial, managerial, professional and clerical work. This adds up to a massive organizational change and rapid strategic innovation in an area which has generally changed very little over a long period.

This chapter examines the process of initiating and managing new office technology projects and explains why necessary strategic change needs momentum from the top of the organization. The change process is shown to involve organizational 'politics' because it challenges the status quo and can substantially alter the influence and autonomy of individual managers and departments. A strategy is recommended which provides a framework for implementing the approaches recommended in the rest of the book.

THE IMPORTANCE OF A STRATEGY

The word 'strategy' is often little more than a buzzword. Just as devising lots of plans does not necessarily indicate *good* planning, having a large-scale budget and ambitious ideas is not the same thing as an effective strategy. This has caused problems for many organizations. They may have had sound *tactics* for introducing new office technology, such as pilot projects and selected pieces of equipment, which have led to rapid initial progress but somehow a critical mass has not been built up. Several years later, the organization has found itself back at square one — more pilot projects, more word processors and more electronic mail used in a spasmodic way.

The quality of equipment and service are generally reasonably good from professional vendors with proven track records. Office technology has also usually needed less lengthy and risky software development than have data processing applications. Even so, progress has been piece-meal because a clear strategy for change has been lacking. This has led to:

— a tactical focus on single projects;

— a technocentric view of new office systems as being primarily concerned with equipment to be installed;

— a vague definition of 'productivity';

— the absence of mechanisms for diffusing office technology and integrating it into the organization;

— a lack of management processes to handle the legitimately political nature of strategic innovation.

New office technology has the potential to change the nature of organizational life and cross organizational boundaries. It makes virtually everyone in an organization a direct user of information technology. Office automation will therefore be seen to be disruptive to many of the competing interest groups within an organization. The stakes are high and key decisions cannot be left to relatively junior technical specialists. A growing body of empirical research and practical experiences of implementing office technology have pointed to an emphatic message: *office technology is essentially concerned with organizational change*. Technical tactics are not enough and delegation of responsibility is not a strategy. The most senior management levels must fully accept their responsibilities and take effective and appropriate action.

Basic elements of a strategy
Once senior management is convinced of the potential value of office technology, a *development contract* should be assigned to an individual or group within the organization (see discussion later in the chapter). Senior management must ensure that the contract is well defined and is backed by adequate resources. It must be assigned to a unit that has the necessary mandate, resources and competence to ensure that the computer-based systems provide the intended benefits. Top management must also provide the mechanisms to carry out successful coordination, and co-operation within the organization to expedite delivery of the required system solutions. This can be done, for example, using a steering committee with representatives from all relevant groups (see Chapters 4

and 6). The rest of this chapter identifies the key elements of a strategy by analysing the possible answers to four important questions:

—*development contract:* who gets the assignment?

—*productivity:* what are the corporate or business messages which management provides to justify the office technology 'contract' to its own people and to provide clear guidelines to the implementors?

—*resources list:* are *all* the resources available which are necessary to fulfil the contract, such as skills, people, education and authority, as well as money and technology?

—*phasing criteria:* is there a clear implementation plan, with guidelines for deciding on implementation priorities?

THE DEVELOPMENT CONTRACT

Many organizations have well established Data Processing (DP) departments with responsibility for computers. The DP department may therefore appear to be the 'natural' choice for being assigned the office technology development contract. Its staff has solid technical experience in installing hardware, building software and operating computer-based information services. There are, however, some important differences between office automation and DP developments. Office technology, for example:

—reflects new expectations about the role of information technology in the organization;

—places terminals into job functions that affect organizational 'cultures' untouched by DP;

—implies new reporting relationships, planning practices and investment/ payoff measures;

—involves broad, and often new, development skills, with an emphasis on implementation aspects;

—makes human and organizational 'behavioural' issues a central and critical requirement;

—affects many people, bringing major consequences for jobs, skills, autonomy and authority.

This adds up to a very different set of capabilities and requirements to those typical in DP operations. In DP, the technocentric view tended to predominate, software building was a key priority, the direct effects were felt by a relatively small number of people and behavioural issues could be ignored. The impact of DP was confined to relatively few jobs and levels of the organization. Top management could cope by planning a reactive role, getting involved only in go/no-go decisions. Office technology cannot be easily assimilated into these traditional arrangements. The main differences between the key organizational and management factors in DP and office technology are highlighted in Figure 3.1. Many of these are discussed in more detail elsewhere in the book. An effective office technology strategy depends upon active direction from the top. It is perfectly reasonable, of course, for senior management to decide that the time, effort, new learning and planning required to take an active role are too much for it. In that circumstance, any significant office technology venture is unlikely to work or, at the very least, will create political conflict and disruption within the organization. It is then far better to avoid office technology or limit it to smaller scale tactical activities.

DP or not DP
There can be no general rule about who should be allocated the development contract for office technology. The decision depends on the types of skills available and the experiences within the organization. In 1980, about one-third of major organizations carrying out office technology innovation had allocated the development contract to DP. In one-third of the organizations, the contract was assigned to another existing unit, such as Administrative Services, and in one-third, a new group was created, often called Office Systems. Since then, it appears that DP is increasingly becoming the spearhead for office technology. The main argument *in favour of DP departments* is that they have technical skills and experience of systems planning and project management. Any necessary behavioural skills could be added to the DP base, which may be easier than providing the technical expertise to behavioural specialists. The most frequent argument *against DP* is that DP departments have been physically and psychologically isolated from the main stream of the organization and have become identified with bureaucracy, inflexible systems and unresponsive service. Technical expertise can be obtained from outside, it has been argued, but knowledge of the organization cannot be bought in. Many DP departments' real authority and credibility are not accepted by line managers. The creation of a new group to handle office technology has the advantage that it can be assembled to match the actual requirements of office technology rather

Factor	Focus of changes caused by new office technology
Expectations	— Value-added benefits rather than cost substitution. — New ways of doing jobs versus more efficient performance of existing ones.
User 'culture'	— Hands-on use of terminals by people with no direct experience of computers and/or no prior expectation of using them in their work. — Designers and implementors who are credible throughout the organization and who are capable of leading this cultural change and of reducing culture shock.
Organizational relationships; planning practices; investment/ payoff measures	— Active involvement by managers, units affected by office technology in setting priorities and scheduling and evaluating potential projects.
Development skills	— Organizational and functional expertise, as well as technical, backed by substantial authority and new planning methods.
Behavioural issues	— Acceptance/resistance (see Chapter 7). — Equity and respect for, and response to, legitimate concerns for personnel issues such as job skills, job satisfaction and status. — Negotiation to resolve issues such as disputes, ambiguities, budgets and so on (see Chapters 5 and 9).

Figure 3.1: Key organizational and management aspects of office technology (highlighting differences from DP).

than adapting from an existing, and possibly inappropriate, structure. On the other hand, any new unit has to start from scratch, building its credibility, procedures and contacts. It may prove to be an organizational orphan which nobody takes seriously.

There is no obvious correct choice. Trade-offs need to be made within any given environment between the key determinants of success: the credibility, authority and stable organizational base of the unit in charge of office technology. Having selected an appropriate unit, senior management cannot abrogate responsibility to it on the basis of a vague and flimsy brief.

A CORPORATE MESSAGE FOR OFFICE TECHNOLOGY

Issuing the development contract determines who will lead the drive towards office technology, but not *why*. 'Productivity' is usually the end for which office technology is the means. It is extremely difficult, however, to translate even commonsense definitions of productivity into something specific. What are 'better' planning,' improved' communications or 'more effective' administration? What is a suitable measure of secretarial productivity? Surely not the speed of typing characters or lines, which is frequently used as the criterion.

The traditional economists' ethos of efficiency defines productivity in terms of output/input ratios. For office technology, this translates to cost displacement and office *automation* — doing the same work more cheaply, faster and with fewer errors. It implies that the 'office' is a factory to be routinized and streamlined. Another view is to consider *value-added* benefits, which are concerned with effectiveness rather than efficiency, doing better work rather than the same work better. This approach emphasizes augmenting people's abilities and supporting, rather than automating, their activities (see also Chapter 2). This view of economic efficiency, coupled with a technocentric perspective of the office as factory, can lead to systems which impair the quality of working life and reduce variety and autonomy of work. Many managerial proponents of office technology, such as Paul Strassman of Xerox Corporation, accept this point but stress that even human and organizational aspects of 'productivity' must be translated into quantifiable economic measures.[1]

An operational definition of productivity is the cornerstone of a strategy for office technology. The fact that this is difficult to do in theory is no excuse for allowing productivity to be defined in vague terms in practice. According to a study of 23 published plans and studies in seven American public and private organizations with a major commitment to new office technology, the lack of productivity of white-collar workers was uniformly identified as the main problem being tackled by office technology.[2] Yet only five of the 23 documents presented a set of indices for measuring productivity. At the same time, all documents discuss factors (such as return on investment, scale of investments and application priorities) which depend on having clear productivity criteria.

Specialists involved in applying computer-based systems thrive on words that rarely get defined, such as 'productivity', 'user involvement' and 'top management commitment'. They are used almost as magic spells, as if to use the label is to create the reality. Memos announcing management's commitment to, and paeans in praise of, productivity are of little value unless the commitment is turned into action via a public statement which translates 'productivity' into something concrete and organizationally meaningful.

If the development contract is issued with only vague justifications about productivity and other goals, people will have to decipher the objectives for themselves. This is likely to lead to a variety of interpretations of the motivations behind the development and entirely different perceptions of the future. Management should therefore specify and communicate coherent and clear corporate/business messages. This applies to private and public organizations, although the 'business' of a public organization usually has different goals and priorities to the profit-orientation of private companies; questions of efficiency, productivity, customer/client service, and other impacts of office technology are of relevance in both environments.

The corporate/business message should include the following:

— *The need for change:* why change is necessary; where the organization is going; what the opportunities and problems are in relation to, for example, the organization's political, social, economic and competitive environment; what the 'critical success factors' are (the key things the system must do well)[3]; what plans have been developed for growth or retrenchment, new services and organizational restructuring.

— *Definition of 'productivity':* what office technology is intended to contribute.

— *Commitments by and to Management:* what priority is given to office technology; who is in charge, with what mandate and what authority; what management expects from staff at all levels in terms of involvement, planning and implementation.

— *Guarantees:* change inevitably involves a degree of stress, so all levels of staff should be offered some guarantee and security, such as a statement that the aim is to have no compulsory layoffs. If staff levels do have to be reduced, this will be done through attrition by natural wastage or through agreed redundancy payments (see Chapter 9).

The corporate/business message is critical. If 'productivity' cannot be expressed in the above way, how can office technology investments really be justified and productivity gains demonstrated? If no clear explanation of the context for office technology is given and guarantees made that people will not lose from the stresses and consequences of change, how can workers commit themselves to the strategy or understand what it implies? If the issuing of the development contract for office technology — whether to DP or any other unit — is not accompanied by a clear mandate and justification, why should capable, busy line managers and supervisors defer to a group for which they see little legitimacy? And if management cannot write a coherent corporate 'business' message, it is hard to see why it should get involved with office technology at all.

Management and staff resistance

The possible resistance of secretarial and clerical staff to office technology innovations is examined in many places in this book, for example in Chapter 7. Resistance can also occur among managers who object to the kinds of intrusion into their territory which are a natural consequence of office technology change[4]. Technical experts also guard their own domains.

Employees rarely think of 'productivity' as such. Instead they tend to think of work improvements in terms like 'doing a good job' or of their organization as 'a good place to work'. When looking at strategic innovation, they naturally want to know what it will mean for their particular jobs and what it will be like to work in the organization in the future. 'Productivity' is often regarded as a code word for redundancies and/or major changes in work practices; even talking about the need for it can sound like a criticism of existing performance. Perhaps there should be a moratorium on using the word 'productivity'.

The picture built up of the intentions for and likely consequences of introducing new office technology determines the response of people in the organization. The corporate/business message should help to build an accurate picture. This may still result in some resistance but at least it will be informed resistance. It is unreasonable to expect everyone to accept the many and varied changes which office technology implies for jobs, working relationships, career growth, supervision, and so on.

Evidence from studies of the introduction of new technologies strongly indicates that change must be self-motivated and that innovation is driven by *value* not cost[5]. If there is no value, any cost is disproportionate. The 'felt need' is of importance in the implementation of computer systems and the 'unfreezing' of an organization is required to create a momentum for change. Office technology plans which leave productivity undefined, focus on equipment and technical issues, and emphasize secretarial and clerical efficiency do provide a clear picture — perhaps even the one management intends. Resistance to such a picture, however, seems a very rational response.

RESOURCES NEEDED FOR OFFICE TECHNOLOGY INNOVATION

Six basic types of resources are needed to implement computer-based office systems:

—hardware;

—purchased software;

—technical development staff to build tailor-made 'applications' software, databases and networks;

—managers, staff and methods for project control;

—implementation support staff;

—business/corporate planners.

If office technology innovation is to avoid reliving the truly awful early history of DP, care should be taken to provide adequate resources in *all* these categories. Some office technology projects, however, have exhibited the same major failing of many DP ventures, which is to have an over-emphasis on hardware and technical design in budgets and plans. This makes it appear that the main objective is to install equipment, rather than to implement broader changes. Schedules are then likely to be accelerated because the hardware is available and most office technology software is provided by the vendor. In the haste, implementation support is neglected.

During the 1960s, almost the whole of the DP budget was taken up by hardware, software and specialist staff; in those days, hardware costs were much higher than for personnel and software (see Chapter 1). As hardware costs fell, DP staff salaries and software costs rose which shifted the emphasis to software. When it was realized in the 1970s that DP systems were frequently unsuccessful, demand grew for resources to manage and implement project controls. Implementation support staff and business planners, however, were ignored for a long time.

Gradually, the emphasis has therefore shifted from equipment and design to implementation; from making a system work technically to making it work in the context of people, jobs, organizational structures and work flows. A key element is handling the 'culture gap' between users and designers. This requires the participation of 'hybrid' individuals, who are fluent about the technology and literate about its application. Most studies of successful implementation of computer-based systems shows the importance of skilled hybrids: facilitators, change agents, educators and consultants[6]. The studies of unsuccessful efforts attribute the negative consequences of a technocentric design focus to user departments which had no way to support the user and bridge the culture gap.

The need for business and corporate planners to be involved in computer-based systems was also highlighted by computing failures. Many DP managers lost their jobs in the 1970s because there was no link between the corporate/business plan and the computing plan. When information technology became more important to organizational effectiveness and very survival, a new 'breed' of DP manager emerged with the skills and expertise to run the DP unit in a way which could meet corporation *and* technological objectives. The need to provide adequate business and corporate planning resources is even more important with office technology.

Supporting the introduction of new systems
Office technology need not follow the awful history of DP, but it will if implementation and corporate/business planning resources are inadequate. Office technology should not be parachuted into user

departments as happened with some DP systems. It should be phased-in with careful attention paid to organizational issues and with increasing effort going into making 'user involvement' real, instead of having pseudo-participation, and training should become more than a casual add-on to development.

Technical components can be installed in a few weeks with the capability of replacing executives' secretaries with word-processing centres, terminals for electronic mail and dictation machines. The executives cannot adjust so quickly, however, although they are often quite ready to sanction major and rapid changes in how their subordinates' jobs are done. The executives' feelings are often ones of fear, uncertainty and resistance. They need support. Any organization foolish enough to try to automate such a manager's office at short notice will quickly learn the difference between installation and implementation.

The main types of implementation job functions are:

— *facilitators* who understand the user's jobs and the technology so that they can prepare users for change and provide a basis for mutual understanding between users and technicians. In Chapter 4, Enid Mumford discusses the role of a facilitator in relation to staff participation in system design, but facilitators are also required to support changes in managerial and professional roles;

— *teachers* who not only train people to operate equipment but who can also help users adapt to the system and the system to adapt to a user's special needs and context;

— *consultants* to answer questions, troubleshoot and give advice.

The people who can carry out these functions require 'hybrid' skills. Such people must be credible to users, good communicators, and specialists in understanding the technical tools.

Significant resources must also be allocated to corporate/business planning because office technology projects intend to affect every major aspect of text handling and communications. At some stage 'text handling' and 'communication' must be translated into operational objectives like customer and client service, personnel administration, financial reporting and market management. If office technology is to make an effective impact on the 'productivity' issue, it is important and useful to understand both corporate and user problems and to provide

long-term planning and liaison between the office technology development and other relevant operational units within the organization.

The use of outside consultants

The resource list for office technology spans a wide range of needs and
skills; many of these skills are in short supply. It is therefore often
necessary to call in outside consultants. Consultants can contribute ideas
and new insights, provide special expertise, or perform specific tasks. In
most cases, they cannot take a leading role in areas, such as office
technology, that require legitimacy within the organization, authority
and a stable internal base in order to be effective. Key staff for
implementation support should usually come from within the organization. In a new and expanding field such as office technology, professional
qualifications and abilities of consultants are hard to judge. Consultants'
disadvantages often tend to become obvious *after* their work has been
completed. Consultants can, however, be an asset provided the organizations consider the following guidelines, based on comments from senior
executives who have successfully launched strategies for office technology:

— potential consultants should be analyzed in terms of three main
  categories: doers, ideas people and advisers;

— perceptions of the role of the consultant should be carefully managed
  to overcome a naturally anti-consultant attitude amongst many
  people;

— the office technology leader must build and manage the relationship
  with the consultant;

— consultants must never be used in areas that involve internal politics;

Figure 3.2 summaries how the different types of consultant can contribute
to the activities covered by the resource list. *Doers* are the solid
professionals who can take over discrete tasks with clear objectives that
can be delivered. They do what they are told, have well defined codes of
good practice and require (and respond to) clients who know what they
want. *Ideas people* are very different. They need to assist with innovation,
invention and the breaking away from old concepts. They must provide
first-rate imaginative and intellectual inputs. Good ideas people may,
unfortunately, be hard to distinguish from mediocre ones armed with
phrases and frameworks: good ones should have a proven track record
and prefer to build up long-term relationships with clients, usually via
key contacts within the organization who can guide them and use their

ideas. *Advisers* are especially useful in providing the equivalent of a doctor's second opinion, particularly in the review process. They do not expect long-term or close relationships with clients.

Resource Category	Doers	Ideas People	Advisers
Hardware	Installation	Strategic thinking	Selection, review
Purchased software	Installation	—	Selection, review
Development staff	Contract work	Innovative design	Design review
Project control	—	—	Progress review
Implementation support	Training material	Implementation strategy	Progress review
Business planning	Forecasting, market analysis	Strategic thinking	Review

Figure 3.2: Roles that can be carried out by Consultants.

LEADERSHIP AND AUTHORITY: THE MISSING RESOURCE

The resource requirements discussed in the previous section encompass the financial, technical and human capital needed for the office technology development contract. There is another category — *authority*, and its correlate *leadership*, which are the organizational capital which mobilizes the other resources. The development contract has to include a specific mandate and the authority to make it work.

Many of the 'political' fights over computing resources are really arguments about *who* decides, not what to decide. In the early 1970s, it was hardly a resource worth fighting over in terms of budget, territory and value to the organization. Office technology, however, can be a battleground on all three accounts. One of the main conflicts is between the centralized approach traditionally taken by DP and the desire for local autonomy over office technology. Word processors, networked information services, software packages and contract programmers can be obtained from a range of sources. This has broken the previous monopoly of computing resources, which was held by DP.

In many companies, office technology got off the ground through local initiatives. In others, DP has tried to maintain its monopoly by preventing, for example, the acquisition of microcomputers or computing services from independent companies outside the organization. There are strong arguments which support having both a central direction and local autonomy for all computing services. Local autonomy ensures that individual units can set their own priorities and get the needed benefits quickly, avoiding any DP bottlenecks. Central direction, however, is essential to guarantee future stable integration of data and communications and to avoid fragmentation and duplication of effort.

It makes no sense to give responsibility for office technology to a unit that does not have the authority. At the same time, giving authority to an individual to lead office technology is not enough in itself. He or she must have the experience, personality and credibility to use it effectively. The characteristics of a 'good leader' in office technology are likely to be similar to those of the *innovator*, which are to focus on problem solving, have a high credibility which allows risks to be taken, and a degree of hard-nosed pragmatism which prevents extreme risks. Innovators are different to ideas people. Innovators focus their energies on results, show a readiness to seek out new ideas and know how to use ideas people.

If the authority for office technology is assigned to DP, the leadership of DP should be in the hands of the new breed of DP managers, who are innovators, anxious to build a service image within the organization, and who attract senior management attention and make a visible commitment to corporate/business performance. The traditional type of DP managers, however, would fail to provide effective leadership because they focussed too much on DP operations rather than corporate activities, were narrow-minded, did not think sufficiently in terms of service, and were not viewed with respect by line managers.

Once office technology affects key aspects of the organization — or at least tries to do so — it will need the co-operation of senior line managers. The questions of mandate, authority and leadership will then become central.

It can be easy to overlook the need for these non-traditional resources if office technology is viewed primarily in terms of its means (hardware and software) rather than its ends (major organizational change). Only top management can create the mandate and authority but it may not find it easy to identify the right innovator. A major reason against giving the development contractor to a particular unit could be that its head would not be able to provide the appropriate innovative leadership, even though the unit has been given the right mandate and authority.

PHASING THE GRAND PLAN: WHAT COMES FIRST?

One of the clearest conclusions from research into the implementation of office automation is that effective change occurs only at an evolutionary, rather than revolutionary pace. Ambitious 'all-or-nothing' projects with a delivery date many years in the future rarely work. Organizations should not shrink from setting ambitious goals for office technology but these should be achieved in a phased manner. The evidence suggests the following.

— If a project cannot be phased, it is unlikely to work.

— The initial phases establish credibility and value.

— The early phases are essential for learning and for evolving a fuller design, particularly if the organization has no previous experience of office technology, and cannot schedule what is really an invention.

— Phasing hedges risk. In the all-or-nothing approach, the system will either work or not work and the organization will have spent a lot of money before it finds out. Phasing ensures that if anything goes wrong, the organization can back out, re-evaluate the design and also have the practical benefits from any earlier phases.

Office technology should learn the lesson well of early DP, where phasing was non-existent. It was as if an aircraft manufacturer introduced a new state-of-the-art aeroplane without testing out models or using simulations. Phasing, however, must have a long-term goal, incorporated into the corporate/business message if it is to be successful. Otherwise, phasing will result in a haphazard series of unco-ordinated experiments.

RECOMMENDATIONS

1 Top management *must* play an active role in office technology by:

— agreeing, defining and making public a coherent strategy;

— placing a development contract with an internal unit that has a strong mandate, authority and innovative leadership capability;

— producing a corporate/business message with realistic and clear guidelines on what productivity improvements are expected;

— ensuring that *all* necessary resources are available, particularly those concerned with implementation support and corporate/business planning;

— specifying phasing criteria that are aligned to corporate objectives.

2 Be aware that office technology means more than just bits and pieces of equipment. It is an aggressive mission that intends, and relies on, organizational change and a complete redefinition of jobs, relationships and roles at work.

3 Limit or abandon office technology developments if top management are unable or unwilling to commit themselves to an active role. If the office technology tactics involve small applications and do not affect mainstream corporate activities, many of the potential problems will not occur. This means that there will, at best, be small economic gains and no real productivity improvements, which raises doubts about what could be a waste of money, albeit a relatively small investment compared to more important new systems.

4 Prepare a strategy for top management to resolve political infighting within the organization, say between DP and other units for control of office technology.

5 A corporate plan for integrating all information technology applications should be developed.

6 Select with care people with 'hybrid' technical and corporate/business skills to support the introduction of new technology (such as facilitators and teachers).

7 Decide where and how outside consultants are to be used.

8 Ensure the strategy explicitly defines how all levels of staff can participate in the change process and what guarantees can be provided regarding the inevitable fears and uncertainties felt by many employees.

9 Pinpoint the phased activities within the corporate/business plan. The initial application(s) should:

— be *self-justifying*, clearly seen to contribute to productivity in terms of the long-term corporate/business plan, not dependent on elaborate cost-benefit calculations;

— *make someone happy* by solving a problem or creating an opportunity for some group or individual in the organization;

— be *phaseable* with clear deliverables and short phases (one to three months);

— *teach* designers and users how to extend or improve the quality and scope of office technology;

— *not put at risk* the morale, efficiency and stability of the user organization.

REFERENCES

1 Strassman, P., 'Managing the Costs of Information', *Harvard Business Review* (September-October 1976).

2 Molson, K., 'A Strategic Planning Framework for Office Automation', Sloan School of Management, Massachusetts Institute of Technology, MASS, Unpublished Master's thesis (1980).

3 Rockart, J.F., 'Chief Executives Define Their Own Data Needs', *Harvard Business Review,* (March-April 1979).

4 Keen, P.G.W., 'Information Systems and Organizational Change', *Communications of the ACM* (January 1981).

5 Keen P.G.W., 'Value Analysis: Justifying Decision Support Systems', *MIS Quarterly,* (Spring 1981).

6 Keen, P.G.W., Meyer, N.D., 'Implementation Techniques', *Diebold Automated Office Program Report* (1979).

CHAPTER 4: SUCCESSFUL SYSTEMS DESIGN

Enid Mumford

INTRODUCTION

The creation of a successful information system involves the design of social and organizational activities as well as technical aspects. The systems design process, however, is often viewed primarily as the development of a technical specification. The failure to give sufficient attention to non-technical objectives is likely to mean that there is a poor match between the characteristics of the system and the needs of the employees and organizations who use it.

This chapter describes how different approaches to systems design produce varying human consequences and overall effectiveness. It places current attitudes to systems design in an historical perspective to illustrate the underlying values which play a crucial role in shaping the implementation of new technology. A strategy for office systems design is recommended, which synthesizes organizational, human and technical requirements.

DESIGN OF COMPUTER-BASED SYSTEMS

The design of computer-based systems in the office and on the shop floor has frequently been regarded as the responsibility primarily of computer technologists. This has led to a technically-dominated (*techno-centric*) view of the objectives and impact of the system. As illustrated in Chapter 2, such a partial view results in an inefficient system. It also undervalues human skills and abilities. The aim of such a technical approach is to reduce human intervention to the minimum; skill, control and judgement are built into the machine wherever possible.

This follows the tradition of *scientific management* which dominated the design of manufacturing automation during the first half of the twentieth century. The approach was first articulated in the 1830s by

Charles Babbage, the British inventor of the computer. An American engineer, Frederick Winslow Taylor, developed similar ideas and became a key proponent of scientific management, which is sometimes called Taylorism. He aimed to apply 'rational' intelligence and scientific method to sort out what he saw as muddle and inefficiency in industry.

Taylor believed that management's main role was to study the best methods for carrying out tasks and for measuring the level of perform-ance. The role of the worker in his view was to obey management-defined procedures and to be rewarded if clearly defined targets were met. He also emphasized a concept that has been widely adopted in computer-based systems — the separation of 'doing' from 'thinking and planning'. Workers did things, but management, he believed, was responsible for thinking and planning.

With information systems, management has tended to delegate plan-ning and design responsibilities to specialist systems analysts. Although the analysts often work within the user organization, they are 'outsiders' and independent from users of the system. According to Tayloristic theory, this gives them an 'objectivity', which is desirable in manipulat-ing and determining the quantifiable, measurable and controllable system techniques and criteria that provide a 'rational' working environment.

Computers first — users last

The nature of early computer systems encouraged technical designers to focus more on the needs of the computer than the broader organizational and human factors. An information systems specialist, Harold Sackman, explained the development of the technical systems analyst ethos as follows:

> Early computers were virtually one of a kind, very expensive to build and operate. Computer time was far more expensive than human time. Under these constraints, it was essential that computer efficiency came first, with people last . . . Technical matters turned computer professionals on; human matters turned them off. Users were trouble-some petitioners somewhere at the end of the line who had to be satisfied with what they got[1].

During this formative era of computing, Sackman observed that the user was forced into a 'subservient attitude towards the almighty machine'. He found that this attitude was transmitted from pioneer designers of computer systems to their disciples.

Sociologist Ida Hoos was one of the first people to draw attention to the dangers of believing that people from outside an operational system have an advantage as designers over people from inside. In 1969 she wrote that systems analysis techniques implied that social systems could be reduced to measurable, controllable units all of whose relationships are fully recognized, appreciated and amenable to manipulation. She commented:

> Justification for this line of thought appears to be vested in the belief that experts from outside the discipline will bring to the problem a fresh approach, unfettered by doctrinaire restraints . . . In practice none of these has found substantiation. Reviews of completed systems analyses indicated that, far from submitting gracefully to quantitative treatment, social systems are by their very nature so laden with intangible, human variables that concentration on their measurable aspects distorts the problem and confuses the issues. I would suggest that instead of assuming that social systems should be approached as though readily subject to technical treatment, those which appear technical might more appropriately be treated as social in their essence[2].

A more balanced view of reality

In a situation where the potential users of the system are insufficiently involved in the development process, the systems designer is left to create the organizational 'reality' that defines the functions performed by the computer. The designer's perception, however, may not coincide with the reality as seen by the managers and workers who have to operate the resultant system.

My own practical research clearly indicates that explicit human and organizational objectives must be set at the outset as well as technical and economic goals. The principal factor determining whether comprehensive objectives are set is the values of influential key groups. If either top management, systems designers or users recognize the need to design systems which combine social and technical requirements (called *socio-technical*) and can get their views known and accepted, then organizational and human objectives are usually set and achieved. Where management or technologists are not concerned with human needs and users are passive or powerless, only technical and short-term economic objectives are usually set; even where these are achieved, the system often fails to satisfy crucial social and long-term economic requirements, which often had never even formed part of the technical brief.

Examples of successful and unsuccessful design

Many examples are given in this book of systems that failed although they worked technically (see, for instance, Chapter 2). The following, taken from my own studies, illustrate the different results that can be achieved by adopting alternative approaches. The first two examples followed the traditional technical systems analyst method and the other two are socio-technical designs.

* A government unemployment department decided to pay claimants via a computer at a central office rather than through clerks in local branch offices. The system objectives were set by a technical design group in a central office many miles from the branch offices. Although few major changes occurred in the structure of work within the branches, the computer was viewed with great hostility by the staff who had to work with it. The computer seriously interfered with the most valued aspect of their work — their ability to provide a direct expert service to the public and to know that the public recognized and appreciated this service. With the computer, they simply identified that the person had a valid claim then passed details to the computer. There were frequent delays in payments. The public would complain to the local office about such delays but the clerks had little control over improving matters. Eventually the staff had to be put behind security barriers to protect them from the sometimes violent public.

* A savings bank introduced a computer system to reduce costs (mainly through staff reductions), improve efficiency and provide a better service to the public. After implementation, clerks said they no longer had opportunities to get a 'sense of achievement' from work or to experience 'enjoyment'. This was because top management and systems designers never considered using the system as a vehicle for redesigning work to improve job satisfaction, in addition to the other objectives (see also Chapter 7).

* In another bank, an increase in job satisfaction was made a specific objective when a computer was introduced to assist the foreign exchange department. The reason was that the bank was experiencing some difficulties in attracting and retaining staff. The bank clerks themselves were made responsible for designing an optimal form of work organization into which the computer system could be fitted. This was achieved successfully.

* At the Aero Engine Division of Rolls-Royce in the UK, a consensus

approach was chosen in order to ensure that the system would be acceptable to staff who were to operate it, as well as meeting other objectives. A representative group of clerks who formed the design team was able to suggest a number of alternative forms of work organization. The work structure chosen by a majority of staff was implemented and produced more efficiency *and* a higher level of job satisfaction.

HOW TO APPROACH SYSTEMS DESIGN

A necessary component of the successful creation and survival of computer systems is a definition of the environmental reality which is jointly agreed by the systems designer and the system users. This similarity of perception, if it can be achieved, should produce an effective match between the efficiency needs of the enterprise, which must be met if it is to survive, and the human needs of those workers and managers who use the computer.

The role of the technical designer

The attitudes of technically-oriented systems designers are usually influenced by a strong allegiance to technology, which affects the way they see the world and their design responsibilities. An over-simplified conception of how people behave enables the designer to concentrate on the complexity of technology without having to spend a great deal of time considering the complexity of human beings. When the system is finally implemented, the discounting of human factors in the original 'model' means that the system can be evaluated merely in terms of its technical rather than socio-technical achievements.

The designer, of course, is creating not just a technical system but an organizational world and the rules by which it will operate. By simplifying and reducing variety in the system's model, the designer is likely to create a fantasy world, which bears little similarity to the world of the users of the system. Designers do not do this consciously. In fact, they often view their own jobs as heroic struggles to meet what they see as user needs.

In this 'heroic' role, the designer feels faced with technical and social obstacles in winning approval for his or her concept. The designer-hero's vision is of a world in which mountains of data may require scaling. Micro-seconds of precious computer time may separate success from failure. Impossible schedules may be demanded, and organized opposition may be lurking in the wings to 'shoot down' design plans[3]. I have seen a sign above the desks of a team of systems designers which said: 'If it works, it is obsolete.' Design is seen as heroic but implementation and maintenance is dull. The systems designer is unwilling to share the most interesting heroic aspects of the design and so encounters trouble with the managers who implement systems and the people who have to use them.

The solution should lie in making system design a joint venture in which managers, supervisors, implementors, users, operators and others with an involvement in the system participate. They could all share in the adventure of designing a system. Such a joint approach, however, tends to reflect a value system which is very different from that adopted by the technical designers or proponents of scientific management.

Technically-oriented computer system design has not been consciously derived from Taylorism. Most designers have probably never heard of Taylor or scientific management. But there is a close correlation between the types of job design that result from both approaches, even though the technical designer is often unaware of being a job designer as well as a technical specialist.

Two researchers who hold a strong humanistic value position, Robert Boguslaw and Louis Davis, have clearly described the impact of a Tayloristic technical design methodology on the working environment. According to Boguslaw, the designers are concerned with 'non-people and people substitutes'. The theoretical and practical solutions call for decreases in the numbers and scope of responsibility of human beings within the operating structures of their new machine systems[4]. Davis believes that the technical designer has no clear objectives concerning roles for people as people, but that objectives are clearly defined for people as machines. When technology is translated into requirements for job designs, Davis has seen widespread acceptance of the notion of a 'technological imperative' in which the demands of the technology are regarded as paramount[5].

The rise of rationalism
Technical systems design and Taylorism are manifestations of a rationalist philosophy which was first made explicit in the writings of eighteenth-century philosophers and economists. It was based on a belief in human development and progress in which greater knowledge could lead to greater happiness. These ideas were given practical form by engineering

innovations which led to the Industrial Revolution and the growth of large-scale industrial organization.

Rationalism evolved by transferring to secular thought many ideas derived from the quest for truth which had dominated religious thinking in Europe. The desire for human redemption was reformulated to lead to the goal of rationality, a drive to classify and quantify and to promote the dominance of order and control. Newtonian physics was seen as a framework for developing various kinds of social systems and inspired Adam Smith, who founded economics as a science in 1775, to publish his *Wealth of Nations*.

At about the same time, utilitarians such as Jeremy Bentham strove to maximize material happiness. Bentham believed that wealth produced an equivalent amount of happiness. He wanted to establish morals as an exact science and subject it to the rule of reason. Whereas the later work of Taylor was based on *l'homme boeuf*, the strong man who could be assisted to use his strength to maximise his material prosperity, Bentham was influenced by *l'homme machine*, a man reduced through scientific investigation to determined conditions. In this way, Bentham created the basis of economic planning and social engineering as we know it today.

Technical developments reinforced and gave practical form to these ideas of efficiency, utility and rationality. Inventions like the steam engine showed that technological principles could be applied to large-scale work problems. Engineer and mathematician Charles Babbage not only invented the computer but anticipated its potential impact on work organization. In 1835, Babbage wrote:

> The constant repetition of the same process necessarily produces in the workman a degree of excellence and rapidity in his particular department, which is never possessed by a person who is obliged to execute many different processes. This rapidity is still further increased from the circumstances that most of the operations in factories where the division of labour is carried to a considerable extent are paid for as piece work . . .[6]

At the same time, Karl Marx was writing about the exploitation of the labourer in the factory. Like Bentham, Marx believed in a rational social order, but one of a different kind from that which he saw developing in the capitalist industrialized world. An influential critic of rationalism was Max Weber. His description of the bureaucratic pattern that resulted from the application of rationalization were similar to some

Marxist analyses. But whereas Marx saw the abolition of private property as the cure for workers' alienation, Weber saw rationalization as an integral part of any industrial society, whether capitalist or socialist.

During the latter part of the nineteenth century, the process of rationalization and mechanization began to speed up. This period saw the beginning of mass production in industry and the fragmentation and de-skilling of work previously performed by craftsmen. The scientific management movement emerged from this background, led by Taylor.

The principles of Taylorism

Taylor's intention was in accord with the philosophy of Bentham. Through applying intelligence and scientific method, he proposed to increase the profitability of the enterprise and the earnings of the employee. The stop-watch was Taylor's bible. He split each job into its component operations and timed each of them. This is the essence of scientific management — the systematic analysis of work into the smallest components and the rearrangement of these elements into the most efficient combination.

Taylor's fame was promoted in 1899 when, as a consultant to the Bethlehem Steel company, he taught a worker named Schmidt to treble his productivity rate for shovelling pig iron. Every detail of Schmidt's job was specified. Taylor recognized that a worker who could do this tightly regimented work needed certain mental characteristics. Indicating his attitude to labourers like Schmidt, Taylor wrote, 'One of the first requirements for a man who is fit to handle pig iron is that he shall be so stupid and so phlegmatic that he more nearly resembles an ox than any other type'. Schmidt, however, was not so phlegmatic. He showed enough initiative to build his own house while working for the steel company.

When Henry Ford used scientific management to establish his car assembly line in Michigan in 1914, Taylor's ideas reached their peak. The values embodied in Taylorism have played a major role in influencing the management of work ever since. Taylor's ideas have spread into computer-based systems and are often supported by a trade union view that any kind of work is acceptable providing it is safe, healthy and well paid. Davis has summarized the values and beliefs associated with scientific management as follows:[5]

— the human being can be treated as an operating unit which can be adjusted by training and incentives to meet the needs of the organization;

— people tend to be unreliable, with narrow capabilities and limited usefulness;

— labour is an expendable and easily replaceable commodity to be bought and sold by the organization;

— the end of increased material comfort justifies the means used to achieve it.

With this model of man at its base, jobs defined by a Tayloristic analysis tend to have the following characteristics:

— a limited range of skills is required, possibly just involving a single skill or procedure;

— few demands are made on the individual worker;

— performance targets are clearly specified;

— work is tightly controlled and measured;

— the individual has little, if any, discretion.

When combined with a vision of a world in which technology contributes to more and better rationalization, the design of information systems using new office technologies could lead to a widespread adoption of Taylorism in white collar office work. There are, however, other approaches which challenge this view.

Alternatives to technical rationalism
The ideas of rationalism and scientific management have been consistently challenged. In the nineteenth century, thinkers like Dostoievsky and Nietzche argued that the rationalist approach would lead to false goals. Many psychologists, behavioural scientists and others continued to develop alternatives to the rationalist ethic. A. H. Maslow and Frederick Herzberg, for example, were amongst those who have influenced management techniques based on the notion that people can develop their potential within an efficient industrial society, provided work is organized in a humanistic way.

The role of technology has also been questioned to show that there is no single technologically-determined consequence; there are good and bad uses of technology which depend on the way it is designed and implemented. As Sigmund Freud once commented, to illustrate the double-edged nature of technology: 'If there were no railways to make light of distance, my child would never have left home and I should not need the telephone to hear his voice'. One of the most powerful alternatives to scientific management has been the socio-technical school of systems design. Its overriding objective has been to make work more satisfying for the person doing it while at the same time enabling this person to contribute to a higher level of technical and organizational efficiency.

The concept emerged from a project in the British coal industry in 1949 which was developed by researchers at the Tavistock Institute, London. They recognized that work systems contain both social and technical components and that these two sets of factors must be integrated in the design process. The initial research came about because the National Coal Board was disturbed at the low morale and low productivity in British coal mines. During the project, the research team came across a colliery in South Yorkshire which was using a different form of work organization from the rest.

Instead of having mines organized in shift groups, with each shift responsible for a different task and no communication or shared responsibility between groups, they found that the miners had introduced a work system similar to that found in the pre-mechanized days of mining. The men were organized into small groups, with each group taking responsibility for the entire work cycle of a part of the face and working autonomously with little supervision. These observations and the implementation of this form of work organization in another colliery led to a set of work design principles very different from the Tayloristic philosophy of small tasks, tight controls and little responsibility.

The principles of socio-technical design
One of the leading socio-technical designers, Eric Trist[7] has summarized the main principles formulated at the Tavistock Institute

— the basic design unit is the overall work system comprising a number of logically integrated tasks or unit operations rather than single tasks or operations which form the system;

— the work *group* becomes the primary social unit, not the individual job holder;

—internal regulation of the system is by the work group itself;

—jobs are multi-skilled because the work group, rather than an individual, is the primary social unit;

—greater emphasis is placed on the discretionary as opposed to the prescribed part of work roles;

—people are treated as complementary to machines, not as extensions of, or subservient to, machines;

—work organization is aimed at increasing rather than decreasing job variety.

These principles are still used by practitioners of socio-technical design and have contributed to the development of effective computer-based and other work systems. They have been evolved subsequently by a variety of design methods and tools for socio-technical approaches.

As with Taylorism, socio-technical designs first appeared primarily at shopfloor level in manufacturing industry. Technical computer designers instinctively adopted a scientific management bias in their methods, so socio-technical researchers have had to develop their own techniques for application to computer systems. Design methodologies are described in more detail by Butera and Bartezzaghi in Chapter 6. My own technique provides an illustration of the type of procedures employed. It offers:

—a participative systems design procedure which involves users in the design process;

—a simple methodology which users can acquire quickly and easily to assist their design participation by helping them carry out the systems analysis and organizational design tasks;

—advice on how to create a participative structure which enables users and technical designers to share decision taking over a period of time;

—exercises and video production which provide new user design groups with an appreciation of the nature of the design process they are embarking on;

—a framework of the types of questions that should be asked and answered in developing the system.

This, and other methodologies of the socio-technical school, are different from the traditional technical systems design approach. They require a commitment to a systematic and methodical approach even greater than that associated with technical design because they handle so many more variables.

The promotion of human interests in work and systems design has also been approached through formal management/union negotiations, as discussed by John Evans in Chapter 9. Many aspects covered by negotiated agreements are an intrinsic part of a socio-technical design, such as the number of work breaks during the day and the length of the task cycle. The labour relations, process must therefore be considered together with any socio-technical design. Socio-technical designers often feel that their contribution is constrained because it may help to improve the social system in relation to a given technology, but to be really effective it should also influence the design of the technology itself.

A STRATEGY TO CREATE WELL DESIGNED SYSTEMS

Socio-technical systems design methodologies provide mechanisms which handle *all* the elements involved in a system — economic, organizational, social, personal and technical. When this is combined with design participation by users of the system, there is also more likely to be a good *fit* between the users' own problems and needs and the social and technical characteristics of the new system. The notion of 'fit' is an important one because it is the reason why some systems are acceptable to users and others are not. Trying to get the 'fit' right also enables a variety of solutions to be adopted, some of which could be similar to a Tayloristic design but which would be welcomed rather than resisted by employees. A Tayloristic kind of work system, with small, specialized jobs and much routine work, may fit very well with the needs of a group of people who happen to like simple, undemanding work and wish for neither personal development nor mental stress in the work environment. Another group, however, may want work with a great deal of challenge, autonomy and self-management.

The problem for a design team that does not involve users is knowing with any accuracy what the needs and problems of its client group really are. Often users themselves do not understand these with any clarity until they have spent some time thinking systematically and analytically about them. The expert group that designs on the basis of 'good guesses' or superficial interviews with users runs the risk that its design solutions will be rejected whether they are based on the ideas of Taylor or the socio-technical school.

The responses of all levels of users — managers and professionals as well as secretarial and clerical — to new office technologies will be positive or negative depending on the extent to which the individual believes that the system assists or conflicts with his or her personal interests. Acceptable systems are created if they are designed on the basis of a good knowledge of what the individual and group interests are and with an understanding of exactly what people are afraid of and why, even when those fears are generated by ill-informed hearsay and emotion. The design group, whether or not it involves users, must be able to show that the technology is not invariably deterministic and that it can be controlled and manipulated to fit the requirements of particular organizational and work environments.

The socio-technical approach is recommended because it is more comprehensive, more adaptable and more likely to fit an organization's needs than a purely Tayloristic or technical method. It encompasses work design that is similar to scientific management analysis where it is appropriate. It also makes more effective use of the skills of the technologist, who can concentrate on developing technical options which meet the goals specified by those with a better understanding of social and work practices.

TRANSLATING DESIGN PHILOSOPHIES INTO WORK SYSTEMS

Systems design practice must be able to operate from a broad base and encompass a number of activities which are either being carried out concurrently or sequentially.

Figure 4.1 suggests a way of approaching the systems design task. This identifies four discrete stages in the design process which should be given equal weight. It is particularly important to tackle the diagnosis phase thoroughly. Good diagnosis is the foundation of good system design. This will mean spending longer on diagnosis but less on design because the design objectives will be clearer and less likely to change subsequently.

With good diagnosis and participation from users, the system should have a long life cycle and match real world requirements. Where these elements have been ignored or dealt with superficially, the phenomenon of 'second-time round' design frequently occurs. A system is designed and installed but problems are found in its operation. Then the whole system has to be redesigned, but this time at a greater cost and within constraints imposed by past investment in equipment, systems and training.

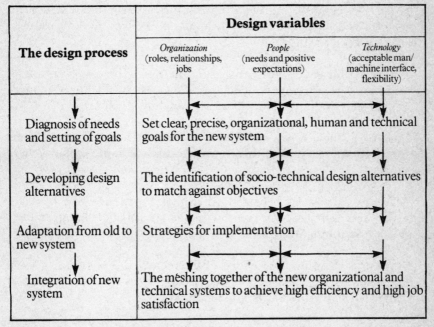

Figure 4.1   A recommended approach to systems design

Goals should be developed and made explicit for each of the major design variables:

— *organizational factors* such as management and work roles, organizational structures, relations within the organization and with the outside world, job design and work practices;

— *human requirements* such as the need for job satisfaction, motivation and positive expectations;

— *technology* which meets organizational and human objectives, such as being flexible, adaptive to changing user environments, with high quality user/system interactions.

The approach in Figure 4.1 is in contrast to technical computer systems design where the technical part of the system is seen as an entity in itself and the sole responsibility of professional systems designers, which is misleading because all working environments contain social and technical elements.

User participation in design

The involvement of users in the design process will help to ensure the creation of acceptable and well-functioning organizational structures that users will welcome. Such participation is likely to contribute to overall success because:

— users can be involved in analyzing their own job satisfaction and efficiency requirements. They are likely to do this analysis more accurately than a group of external technical experts;

— users feel they have a stake in the system because they have some control over their own future work situations and the form these take;

— the design process becomes a learning experience which makes users increasingly competent in the management of change in their own environment;

— an understanding is provided of the technical and organizational characteristics of the new system that enables it to be operated at high efficiency once it is implemented.

The methodologies based on some form of participation require decisions to be taken on how and when to involve users. The technical systems analysis procedure involves managers and users but usually in a passive role and only at the initial stages where they are 'interviewed' by the analyst to find out their formal requirements. Participative design requires a more direct and continuous involvement from users and a sharing of responsibility with the technical designer.

If participation is used as a design strategy, it is essential that the user design group is assisted by someone, called a *facilitator*, who understands both organizational design and the way groups function. The facilitator helps the design team to progress through the different stages of design tasks and keeps them motivated and interested. The facilitator role is important and demanding and is best carried out by a person who has no vested interest in the system but who is skilful in managing social processes. An outsider or member of the personnel department can often fill this role effectively. Courses in skills training can be useful but the best training for a facilitator is undoubtedly experience. Working with design groups over long periods of time provides an understanding of the problems that such groups may encounter and also the available ways of resolving these.

The use of video and other communications media
A new design group is faced with a task of which it may have little understanding and experience. Methods should therefore be explored to communicate to such groups how others in the same situation have managed similar design processes. Video and film can be an effective way of carrying out this communication.

When a new design group is set up, its members should be given a course on design, which takes into account the processes and variables summarized in Figure 4.1. The group should be shown a video or film of a design group 'diary' of the progress of a live project using similar design principles. For example, the video could show a group of secretaries designing the organization of a new word processing system. Video or film is also valuable as a means for communicating information about technical and organizational options that could be considered as part of its members' deliberations and also for informing managers, technologists, trade unions and other interested groups about the progress of the system and the nature of the design process.

RECOMMENDATIONS

1 Ensure that the design process explicitly examines and meets organizational, social, personal and technical objectives. The aim should be a work system that assists employees to achieve a level of efficiency: that gives them pride in their work, provides a high quality working environment, and the opportunity to do rewarding and challenging work.

2 Examine the values and methods of socio-technical design and the use of participative methods, as well as technically-oriented design

and Taylorism. Choose the method which will provide the best fit between the organizational and personal objectives and the chosen technological options.

3 Give priority to the diagnosis phase of systems' design. Ask and answer questions relating to the overall system and to particular subsystems, such as:

— Why do we need to change our present methods? What problems can be overcome or opportunities gained by doing so?

— What are the key objectives and tasks of the areas that will be affected by a new system? What *should* the system and the people using it be doing and how does this compare with what they *are* doing?

— Given these objectives and tasks, what are the problems that must be controlled effectively by any new system?

— Given the personal development needs of the staff, what must a new system provide to increase their job satisfaction?

— What future changes are likely to occur in the environment of the new system to which it must be able to respond?

— Having identified key objectives and tasks, efficiency problems, job satisfaction needs, and likely future change, what specific efficiency, job satisfaction and flexibility objectives must be set to guide the design of the new system?

4 Set organizational and social objectives from the outset and integrate them with technical requirements.

5 Ensure that users from all job levels participate directly in the design process.

6 Regard design as a continuing process of evolution.

REFERENCES

1 Sackman, H., *Mass Information Utilities and Social Excellence*, Auerbach, New York, 1971.

2 Hoos, I., *Systems Analysis in Social Policy*, Institute of Economic Affairs, London, 1969.

3 Swanson, B., 'Systems Heroes', *General Systems*, Vol 19, pages 91-95, 1974.

4 Boguslaw, R., *The New Utopians*, Englewood Cliffs, Prentice-Hall, New York, 1965.

5 Davis, L., 'Job Satisfaction Research: The Post Industrial View', *Industrial Relations*, Vol 10, pages 1176-193, 1971.

6 Babbage, C., *On the Economy of Machinery and Manufacturers*, Charles Knight, London, 1835.

7 Trist, E., *The Evolution of Socio-technical Systems*, Ministry of Labour, Ontario, 1981.

CHAPTER 5: IMPLICATIONS FOR THE ORGANIZATION

Michel Crozier

INTRODUCTION

Public and private bureaucracies of the past have been built on hierarchical structures, with a considerable degree of distance and secrecy intervening between the formulation of decisions at the top and their implementation at the local operational level. The logic of computer-based systems, however, encourages open and equal access to information. It forces management to express decision processes and organizational procedures explicitly so that they can be handled by pre-programmed software routines. These new, sophisticated technological means could perturb the very decision-making processes they are meant to assist.

This chapter emphasizes the significance of analyzing and understanding the actual way large private and public organizations work. The importance of progressing gradually, while learning and bargaining within the organization is explained. There is also an examination of the limits of relying on abstract, rather than practical, organizational design.

THE NATURE OF LARGE ORGANIZATIONS

There has been a tendency to view large State and private bureaucracies as an impending threat which will grow if we continue to pursue the 'dream' of technological rationality. If this were true, computers would complete the movement away from traditional, charismatic modes of management and power. A new 'Big Brother' ruling group would then stay in power forever. I believe, however, that the main danger of an indiscriminate use of computers is not so much that it will give power to a *new* 'rationalist' elite, but that the premature enforcement of computing logic on traditional bureaucratic patterns will prevent the flexibility which has made learning and change possible in the past.

Present-day public and private bureaucracies have been left a legacy of archaic organizational and management patterns from the past. This causes great strain because of the disadvantages of these out-of-date methods and structures. Despite these inadequacies, traditional attitudes and practices still have the advantage of allowing for adaptability and variety. The benefits of human social systems are that they are imperfect and always evolving, thus capable of *learning from experience*. The computer, on the other hand, might fit *too well* with the exhaustive controls idolized by bureaucracies which ignore these benefits.

Hierarchy and distance are key elements in bureaucracies. *Hierarchy* makes it possible to subordinate all possible means and subgoals to the broader corporate objectives. Hierarchical structures seem to be indispensible to establish the necessary authority patterns to get things done. *Distance* protects the figures of authority and prevents favouritism. Such top-heavy bureaucratic management methods are not a twentieth-century phenomenon. Total bureaucratic organizations existed to control most activities in Ancient Egypt, the Inca Empire, and the Mandarin system of traditional China. They relied on the services of elitist classes but they did not need modern technologies to implement their control and domination.

Public democratic institutions are built on opposing principles, which include the primacy of the individual. Within private organizations these principles become manifest, for example, in personnel policies which promote job satisfaction and a high quality working environment, trade union representation in organizational negotiations and moves in some countries towards increased industrial democracy (see Chapters 7 and 9).

The pressures of rapid change
The very rapid development of modern societies has increased pressures on all organizations. Abnormal or impaired functioning (*dysfunctions*) and strains develop. The basic patterns of hierarchy and distance, however, make traditional organizational systems poorly equipped to adapt to this situation because they do not facilitate easy communication from bottom up, or even from the top downwards. Such patterns may be in tune with the requirements of a stable social environment, but they are too rigid when change becomes rapid.

Technology provides an impetus for just such rapid change, at a time when economic interactions have become more complex and increasingly volatile. The result is that the bureaucracy becomes a less efficient mechanism. A growing gap occurs between decision-making systems at the top and the intermediate management and bureaucracies. Management offers face-saving but ineffective solutions and produces a vast number of new rules. Complexity therefore becomes less and less manageable.

Many managers and administrators regard computers as a magical solution for coping with the overload of activities and reducing the level of complexity in the system itself. Although computers can indeed provide some much needed technocratic help with the quantitive problems associated with the decision-making process, they are less able to solve qualitative problems.

Decision Support Systems (see Chapter 1) can be developed that enable computers to take account of a variety of criteria, interactions and inputs. They have the potential to be used to explore the demands of all relevant groups concerned with a problem and to examine the consequences of various possible solutions. This *could* help to reduce areas of contention, clarify choices and lessen the need to have traditional bureaucratic structures to enforce decisions. Unfortunately, this rarely happens.

A major problem is that computer techniques require users to make their working processes explicit *(transparent)*, in order to be able to program the system. This prohibits the usual kinds of *ad hoc* adjustments that make it possible for even large bureaucracies to conciliate contradictory demands for, on the one hand, order and consistency to satisfy corporate requirements and, on the other, for adaptability, the full mobilization of human resources, and rapid communications to meet the needs of 'grassroots' management and staff.

Computers clearly could create over-formalized, over-structured secretarial and clerical jobs (see Chapter 7). Similar tendencies can occur in management, professional and supervisory roles, with programmed rules controlling decision making and other organizational processes.

THE NEW LOGIC OF ORGANIZATION REQUIRED BY COMPUTERS

Any new technical breakthrough is initially utilized within the confines of earlier technological and organizational logic. Only much later does the full potential of the new methods gradually emerge. The computer revolution has been no exception. Its extraordinarily broad social and conceptual aspects have actually made it more difficult than usual to discover how to master its development. This is particularly true when the earliest experiences were gained in one type of relatively self-contained environment (data processing) and the same technological principles were then made available on a vast scale in a different area (new office technology).

When computing first started to be used widely in data processing activities, there was an agreed view amongst managers, users, staff and technical specialists about the role of computers. They were considered to be machines and systems with their own internal logic, which would automatically impose new working arrangements and conditions. Although some trade unions challenged management methods of assessing technological innovation, there was a feeling that this new logic could not be seriously questioned. The difficulties that arose were thought to be merely problems of adjustments of the people to their new tasks (with proper training and good strategies to manage change) and adjustments of the economic and social system (with good planning to take account of changes in job requirements and working environments). In practice, however, computers were used as a new tool to solve the problems of the past rather than of the future. Little consideration was given to the key social and organizational innovations that would follow.

Management and supervisory personnel, as well as secretarial and clerical staff, have reacted with fear and resistance when the technology has 'invaded' their territory. Since management tasks are related to information and restructuring of the information system is the first general organizational consequence of the arrival of the computer, it is no wonder that such problems occurred. The attention of technocrats and top management was attracted only when there were concrete experiences to highlight the nature of the difficulties.

Management and supervisory problems
Three main types of problems developed with computer-based systems at management and supervisory levels: curtailment of the margins of freedom of the operational unit manager; the handling of performance rewards and career developments; and changes in the basic tasks of supervisors (see Chapter 8).

In a traditional organizational structure, line managers have a considerable degree of autonomy and freedom in running their units, provided they meet their overall objectives. A computer can be used, however, to analyse the manager's behaviour in considerable detail and the manager's mission can be more strictly defined within preprogrammed guidelines (see, for example, the case of Danish bank manager in Chapter 7). Such impersonal management makes it difficult to develop informal power and authority networks and to consolidate an expertise by learning from the reactions of clients, customers and colleagues within the organization. The streamlining of operations forces lower management to re-orientate their strategies from a narrow, but human, local vision towards an abstract organizational one.

The impact of computer-based systems on performance rewards and career development has arisen from the attempt to use computers to introduce more 'neutral', less 'biased' standardized criteria of 'efficiency' to judge the performance of operational units and of managers and supervisors. Despite the intended neutrality of these criteria, they have been viewed with suspicion, even if they have not outwardly been rejected. This is because they do not allow people to argue their case directly, to use specific examples of their contribution and to play the game of organizational politics independently. Furthermore, the criteria may be liable to manipulation that could bias the outcome.

Computers can radically affect the basic tasks of lower management echelons and supervisors. In traditional organizations, these supervisory levels had two main kinds of tasks: they co-ordinated the results of their functional units with those of others in the organization and were the senior experts on the skills required by the job. A sophisticated use of computer-based systems alters this because it allows more autonomous groups to deal with *all* the tasks pertaining to a particular function, such as handling all needs of a group of customers or clients. Co-ordination by supervisors is less necessary or is completely eliminated because it is achieved at working level without supervisory intervention.

At the same time, the supervisor's technical expertise can also disappear because each worker becomes more specialized than his or her supervisor. The supervisor's job tends to become more managerial, dealing particularly with personnel policies (such as staff training, promotion, grievances and placements) and making operational adjustments to meet managerial goals; or it could be eliminated. Old style supervisors may find it difficult to make such changes. Furthermore, the changes alter the nature of the social system within the organization because it makes the gap between managerial and operational tasks much greater than the previous seniority gap between junior and senior clerks[1].

How computing can disrupt a successful organization

These problems with management and supervisory roles illustrate the complex issues that can arise as the result of introducing computer-based systems; Brian Wynne in Chapter 8 examines other changes in managerial roles in more detail. The following is a concrete example of the impact that computer-based information systems can have on the overall functioning of an organization.

The case concerns a manufacturing firm which tried to use a computer to create an effective management information system for solving a perennial and costly conflict between its sales force and production units. On the one hand, production departments needed to streamline operations in order to cut down unit costs for highly competitive products. On the other, an equally important sales need was to ensure that each customer received quick and regular deliveries. A conflict arose between the demands of a few large customers, whose orders had to be fulfilled at all costs, and the large number of smaller firms whose total orders were equally indispensable but where individual customers were less visible and exerted weaker immediate pressures.

Management commissioned a computer specialist to develop a solution that would help to optimize the production-line planning and control to resolve the conflicting requirements. After several unsuccessful attempts, a good technical solution was installed on an experimental basis in the smallest production unit of the firm. The system worked well enough and was therefore introduced to the main plant. There it proved to be a complete failure — not because technical flaws emerged but because there was an unexpected problem relating to the social system of the plant.

The computer used data collected on the time taken to manufacture one item. This information was used both for regulating the production process and as the basis of calculating the pay of workers. Technically, this was a rational solution. The problem was that it interfered with previous informal, secretive arrangements which had helped both managers and workers.

A tacit agreement between local management, foremen and employees had allowed the 'time-worked' figures to be falsified. Workers at the factory were paid the regionally agreed branch rate but they received more pay than they should have; they felt this was commensurate with the relative importance of the plant and the bargaining strength of their trade union. The transparency introduced by the computer into the information gathering and processing routines meant that this arrangement could no longer be continued.

A subsequent analysis proved that the whole supervisory system at the plant had relied on the arbitrary leeway gained by the supervisors through tolerating the 'cheating' by the workers. The wheels of the entire endeavour were oiled because the secret arrangement enabled all parties to have a margin for negotiation and the potential for making many other subordinate arrangements[2]. Supervisors could use their bargaining power to obtain the co-operation of workers and their willingness to adjust quickly to crisis situations. Conversely, shop stewards were able to maintain a strong influence on the workers, because they were seen to be the workers' natural partners in the constant bargaining with the supervisors. The advantages gained by this secret agreement meant that none of the parties wanted to accept the obvious solution, which would have been to adjust the rates of pay so that they could use the actual hours worked to achieve the required level of wages.

This example illustrates key elements in the maintenance of the successful operation of large organizations:

— *negotiation and bargaining* must be permitted at all levels, with scope for local autonomy;

— *distance and secrecy* within bureaucracies enable some local bargains to be struck which keep local operations running smoothly, although working to procedures that are different to the norms and rules laid down from the top;

— *transparency* introduced by computers can disturb sensitive areas, which affects the operation of the social system (in the above example, transparency of the collecting and processing of production data caused supervisors and shop stewards to lose the capacity to intervene in the local environment).

Of course, people could be trained to accept the new transparency but this will work only if the computer system is designed to meet human and organizational requirements. A more simplistic and quicker remedy has been to impose a technical solution and try to force people to adjust to it. This method could lead to many of the negative affects of computerization discussed in this book.

DIFFICULTIES OF ORGANIZATIONAL ADJUSTMENT

Traditionally, organizations have developed their decision making system by a painful process of hierarchical adjustments, protected by secrecy (people could for example, make mistakes without necessarily being disciplined according to formal criteria) and based on practical learning through trial and error experiences. This process is an *iterative* one — experiences are analysed, resultant lessons are incorporated in the system, further problems are encountered with the adjusted system which is then re-adjusted to take account of new lessons, and so on.

The logic of the computer, however, aims to integrate all information transactions, to eliminate any contradictions and to introduce transparency in information management and decision making. This logic could be incompatible with the traditional trial-and-error process of iterative, phased adjustments. Theoretically, this incompatibility could either lead to a total rejection of the computing demands or a complete management revolution. In practice, however, the basic trial-and-error approach which characterizes the functioning of social systems will lead to a diverse experience of success and failure, the development of new goals and a great deal of learning at a decentralized level.

The disturbing effect of the process of computerization on the managerial system of bureaucratic organizations is obvious and inescapable. Traditional power systems are based on the continual adjustment over time of several echelons of supervisors and managers, who use their control of tasks and their position and status to strike the best possible deal, to maintain their autonomy and to perform adequately. More transparency will upset their customary deals.

Intermediate echelons, whose main asset was to be the indispensable link in the communications systems, will lose influence if the communication process becomes easier (see Chapter 3). If there were no resistance, this could lead to the suppression of many 'buffer' echelons. The traditionally stratified system of organizations, however, could prevent this from occurring; the regrouping of power positions will still, however, upset the traditional balance of power and entail a great many organizational fights. Lengthy stalemates could ensue because this restructuring is incompatible with an inflexible career system which has a completely different logic. These structural contradictions have lead to three major kinds of risk — *system irrelevance, errors,* and an *increase in complexity.*

Risks of system irrelevance, errors and complexity

The danger of the computer-based information system being irrelevant to the real needs of the organization is perhaps the most frequent risk, leading to a great deal of waste and inefficiency. This may happen because the system was developed as a face-saving exercise by management, without any clear objectives for what it should achieve. If no effort is made to check the validity of information input to the system, the old computing adage will apply — Garbage In, Garbage Out (GIGO).

If staff become alienated, or management is afraid to control the quality of information input for fear of antagonizing the people involved, input errors will increase. A management information system that is so clearly irrelevant that it is generally ignored, or its results are treated sceptically, causes little damage other than the considerable waste of resources in developing it in the first place.

A more serious consequence would be if the irrelevance of the system is unrecognized, so that misleading information is used and acted on. Significant errors can be caused when superficial information based on abstract rules leads to a misreading of facts. Computerized management information systems often reinforce the tendency to rely on abstract rules rather than on the more qualitative experiences of practitioners, which are difficult to enter into a computer that prefers quantified data.

A basic problem in large-scale organizations is the distinction between agents out in the field and the people based at administrative offices. A reliance on computers programmed with formalized rules will reinforce the office-based units at the expense of the agents, who are in direct contact with the 'grassroots' feelings of customers, clients and the world outside corporate offices. The result could be that the whole system loses touch with reality. Although this tendency is particularly noticeable in public services, many large private corporations suffer similar symptoms.

Then there are the dangers of complexity. The computer can be an effective aid in relieving the information work-overload caused by increasing complexity. When trying to provide a comprehensive solution while streamlining operations, extremely complex computing solutions have to be developed to take care of the many contradictions and other factors which influence the behaviour of the system. A frequent illusion is that the transparency required by computers will bring simplicity; in fact, it can cause increased complications, as I have already explained. Transparency prevents the solution of local problems on an *ad hoc* basis. It often encourages the bureaucratization of many activities, which is particularly dangerous because it is often associated with the fragmentation of professional and other jobs.

This has led to a search for a solution in the machines themselves. While big systems built around large-scale computers, it has been argued, necessarily entail centralization, mini and microcomputers could help to reinforce local units to bring about a renewal of decentralization[3]. There is no evidence, however, that mini and microcomputers do bring about decentralization or that large-scale systems are incompatible with decentralization[4]. The problems do not lie in the machines but in the software and, ultimately, with the organizational system itself.

The most basic problem to solve is to determine the *limits* of integrated systems and of programmed intervention. Computers force us to face up to the consequences of the dream of a completely streamlined management of activities which could enforce obedience to all its objectives and constraints. Such a dream is inhuman and extremely dangerous. *We do need contradictions*. Not only is perfection unobtainable, but trying to pursue it too strongly will lead to self-defeating results.

PROGRESS THROUGH LEARNING AND BARGAINING

The first and easiest answer to the organizational problems outlined above is to produce an *abstract* organization design which tries to specify the 'best' rational structure and processes for the organization to meet its objectives. This can also be very dangerous because it is based on organizational models of false exhaustiveness and on mechanisms that assume a deductive logic, moving inexorably from goals to means *(goal-means)*, that will prevent the organization and individuals within it from learning by experience. Systems design techniques are available, however, which emphasize real and adaptable organizational needs (see Chapters 4 and 6) rather than formalized and rigid abstract approaches.

Global, all-encompassing views may *seem* to be a necessary starting

point, particularly if the designer tries to meet the computer's requirement of having all elements of a system described to it in exhaustive
detail. This will prove to be a fake exhaustiveness. It is necessarily based
on theoretical and rather vague descriptions of missions whose practical
content has not been analyzed properly because only local agents,
rather than corporate managers and planners, have experienced the
operations of the system. This is one reason why participation of all
levels of users in the design process is important.

Goal-means deductive design tends to freeze formal mechanisms and
prevents the setting of proper conditions for organizational learning. It
also divorces management control systems from any kind of learning.
Experiences with computerized budgeting systems have shown the
practical difficulties of feeding the formal general schemes with strong
empirical knowledge of the system's operations[5]. The result of relying on
a global, formalized system will entail all the dangers of irrelevance, fake
face-saving and growing complexity described earlier in this chapter.

How to avoid organizational problems
I would recommend a completely different approach. Instead of
emphasizing formal abstract organization design, there should be an
emphasis on the positive knowledge of present organizational patterns
of adjustment. Such a starting point would lead to recognizing the
existence of fragmented and not entirely compatible subsystems. It may
be necessary to improve their compatibilities — but then again it may
not be.

The failures and dysfunctions of these subsystems and the basic
regulations on which they depend must be understood. Breakdowns and
other problems caused by overloads must lead to changes in these
regulations. Such problems can be handled by computers without too
costly a change provided that the systems have been designed so that
they can aid learning mechanisms rather than being frozen into a
'perfect' technical solution.

The learning processes of complex organizations, groups within it, their
clients and representatives need to be analyzed and understood to
provide appropriate aids for particular kinds of activity. For example,
Francis Pave has made a notable case-study analysis of the learning
processes that developed because of a wise use of bargaining constraints
by the French railroad authority (SNCF)[4]. It is particularly noteworthy
in view of the many comparable cases of failure. A general computer
system had been installed to optimize the dispatching of railroad cars

over SNCF's territory. Instead of attempting to build the ideal, all-encompassing theoretical solution, a lot of leeway had been left to the personnel at the switch dispatching stations. This discretionary freedom meant that staff did not have to respect the software rules at all times and they could maintain direct relationships with other stations' staff in the dispatching network.

Dispatchers could therefore work out their own adjustments to *ad hoc* needs, within constraints set by a general computer program. Although the degree of freedom was relatively limited, it was a critical factor in the success of the system. Firstly, it kept employees motivated, active and resourceful; secondly, it enabled better solutions than the preprogrammed ones to be learnt. It allowed the system to be sufficiently flexible to adapt to changing future needs. This flexibility helped to resolve the problem of deciding which stations would survive once the optimized system produced its benefits. No clear good choices were obvious when the system was being designed but, by leaving this operational problem open, appropriate human and technical resources could emerge to solve it. Meanwhile, the capability of management, staff, and the system as a whole, to use computers in an innovative manner had been given a chance to improve through practical experience. Choosing the right angle of approach and deciding on the limits of a system's ability to improve particular activities is not as easy as sweeping superficial evaluations would have it. Keen social systems analysis should be a prerequisite to any action. Progress will come about if knowledge is gained in a step-by-step, incremental way. This must be underpinned by an understanding of the types of bargaining processes and organizational interactions needed for the implementation and operation of any policies by large public and private bodies.

DIFFERENCES BETWEEN PUBLIC AND PRIVATE BUREAUCRACIES

So far, I have not systematically stressed any differences between private and public organizations. This is because I believe there are basically no essential differences in terms of the issues that have been discussed. Private organizations have been as susceptible as public bodies to computer failures, as is illustrated by many of the case studies provided in this book (for example, in Chapters 2 and 6). The different kinds of organizations are, however, faced with strikingly different types of problems.

A customary dogmatic view is to emphasize that public organizations cannot, by their nature, adjust as easily as private organizations to changing circumstances because public services are not subject to dynamic market pressures as an instrument of regulation. This view implies that private organizations will naturally find the best possible adjustment to respond to the requirements of new technologies, using computers more 'rationally' and understand its logic more rapidly. The problems of computerization experienced in private companies, however, does not bear out this reasoning. The basic GIGO problem was first identified in the business world. Even where technical success has been achieved, strongly dysfunctional consequences have occurred. For example, too much transparence in the auditing systems has discouraged innovation[6].

The computer does not provide, as was initially assumed, a single best technical or organizational solution. At first computers provoked dreams (or nightmares) of a Taylorian paradise (or hell). In practice, computers have exploded the Taylorian myth that there was a particular optimum, scientific method of organizing work around machines. They can handle a wide variety of different organizational forms around the machine, from extreme Taylorism to participative socio-technical designs. The best method for a particular work environment depends more on the nature of the organizational cultural milieu in which it is introduced, rather than on a quantitative, 'objective' analysis. One method could succeed in one organization but fail in another.

Major constraints within public bureaucracies have tended to be their capabilities for handling information, communication and co-operation activities. The success of Japanese companies has depended mainly on their ability to apply computing power to handling these factors wisely. In making it necessary and possible to tackle these issues, computers may prove to be the beginning of mastering them. Computers could become a great help in reunifying the theories of public and private management.

The vulnerability of democracy to transparency
In democratic countries, public institutions must be more sensitive to different pressures than private companies. For example, they are subject to majority rule yet must also give priority to the protection of individuals. Democratic institutions provide a basic corrective and indispensable complement to the bureaucratic State. Public legislation

and consumer groups can also, of course, provide corrective forces on private companies beyond the pure competitive market forces.

The democratic public system must make continuous adjustments between the often conflicting needs of central and local State bureaucracies and their related democratic institutions. This makes democracy peculiarly vulnerable to the dangers of transparency introduced by computer systems designed to streamline operations and to simplify the system by clarifying it. Transparency, however, makes it impossible to achieve the necessary deals that relieve the political pressure and which frequently rely on secret negotiations, both at top and local levels.

The political system cannot accept an overdose of rationality. Too much transparency is unbearable because people are accustomed to bureaucratic patterns and procedures as a smokescreen to hide local arrangements. Bureaucracy, once it becomes transparent, will lose its value and the political system will have to become more bureaucratic itself, turning to excessive legalism to resolve conflicts.

International organizations fall prey easily to these dysfunctions. International bureaucracies, instituted to implement the political agreements which governments produce, must retain a minimum amount of leeway. An inconsiderate use of transparency could jeopardize their capability of serving their basic purpose — to provide opportunities and expertise for finding co-operative arrangement without being committed to definitive statements.

Conclusion
Public organizations, therefore, have particular sensitivity to some aspects of computerization. Despite this, the same basic conclusions apply to public and private institutions, particularly regarding transparency, which is a key manifestation of the new computer logic. Transparency, like virtue, is highly desirable, but people are not able to endure the great austerity and anguish of too much virtue. An excess of transparency and superficial rationality could overload already cumbersome organizational bureaucracies. Institutions could crumble because of this pressure unless progress is made by the methods outlined in the previous section.

RECOMMENDATIONS

1 Before concluding the strategy for handling any significant computer-based innovation, ensure that prior understanding has been gained of the main mechanisms that regulate the organizational system involved. It is impossible to elaborate a responsible strategy for change without such knowledge. The importance and strength of the following key characteristics of the systems should be considered:

— secrecy and the implications of transparency;
— learning by experience;
— negotiation and bargaining;
— hierarchical structures.

2 Develop a strategy for helping the relevant system and people within it to learn to deal with any increased transparency; provide limits on the creation of excessive transparency in view of the potential social, political and cultural risks.

3 Ensure that innovation is regarded as an iterative, phased process rather than as a 'big bang', all-encompassing project based on an 'ideal' abstract organizational design.

4 Diagnose the organizational echelons, the professional groups and the managerial functions that will have to bear the brunt of the negotiation and bargaining mechanisms that will operate during the learning process.

5 Elaborate a training program which helps all those affected to exploit positively the opportunities made available to them by new information technologies (see Chapter 12).

6 Provide resources for follow-up guidance to ensure that the evolving system can adapt on a trial-and-error basis as it accumulates experience.

REFERENCES

1 Thomas, D., *Les Employés d'assurance Face au Changement*, Thèse de IIIème Cycle, IEP, Paris, 1979.

2 Crozier, M., *The Stalled Society*, Viking Press, New York, 1974.

3 Lussato, B., *Le défi Informatique*, Edition Fayard, Paris, 1981.

4 Pave, F., *L'hypertaylorisme trahi: de l'usage Contemporain de l'informatique dans quelques Sociétés Industrielles et de Services*, Thèse de IIIème Cycle, IEP, Paris, 1981.

5 Danziger, J., Dutton, W., Kling, R., Kraemer, K., *Computers and Politics: High Technology in American Local Governments*, Columbia University Press, 1982.

6 Hayes, R., Abernathy, W.J., 'Management Minus Invention', *New York Times*, August 20 and 27, 1980.

BIBLIOGRAPHY

Recommended reading of relevance to the issues discussed in this chapter, in addition to the above references, include:

Ackoff, R., 'Management Misinformation Systems' in *Information Technology in a Democracy*, Westin, E. (ed.), Harvard University Press, MASS, 1971.

Crozier, M., Friedberg, E., *L'acteur et le système*, Editions du Seuil, Paris, 1977.

Gotlieb, C., Borodin, A., *Social Issues in Computing*, Academic Press, New York, 1973. Missika, J.L., Pastre, O., *et al*, *Informatisation et Emploi*, La Documentation Francaise, Paris, 1981.

Nora, P., Minc, A., *L'informatisation de la Société*, La Documentation Francaise, Paris, 1978; English translation: *The Computerization of Society*, MIT Press, Cambridge, MASS, 1980.

Simon, H.A., *The New Science of Management Decision-Making*, Prentice-Hall, Englewood Cliffs, N.J., 1977.

CHAPTER 6: CREATING THE RIGHT ORGANIZATIONAL ENVIRONMENT

Federico Butera and Emilio Bartezzaghi

INTRODUCTION

Office automation is often presented as a list of machines and applications, while its associated organizational design is frequently viewed as an extension of the technical design. There is an implicit assumption that organizational structures and people are 'soft' elements that can be adapted to the 'rationality' of the automated information services. Machines, however, are not scattered devices but part of a purposeful technological structure. Men are not isolated entities but part of a social system. Organizational structures cannot be adequately encapsulated in simplistic formal descriptions of procedures and quantified analyses of information volumes and transactions.

This chapter examines the nature of organizational design for computer-based office work in more detail than previous chapters. Examples are given of computer-based management information systems which failed because of inadequate social and organizational design. Organizations are shown to be complex entities which need to be carefully analyzed. Guidelines are provided to assist in the design of organizations and job functions for new office information systems.

WHAT NEW OFFICE SYSTEMS CAN LEARN FROM DATA PROCESSING

For many organizations, attitudes to the potential of new office technologies are shaped by experiences of data processing and management information systems which were the dominant applications of computers in the 1960s and 1970s. 'Traditional' data processing was concerned primarily with highly structured information and formalized procedures. Most offices, however, rely on activities which are less predictable, with a great deal of unstructured information coming from a variety of sources. Nevertheless, many of the lessons learnt from problems and failures with data processing systems are equally applicable to computer-aided office work.

The following examples, compiled with the assistance of Adriano De Maio of the RSO Institute and Politecnico di Milano, provide further illustrations to those given in earlier chapters of difficulties that have occurred with computer systems.

* A large chemical plant introduced a computer-based maintenance procedure to help cut the costs of daily maintenance and to 'rationalize' the activities co-ordinated by departmental supervisors. The system worked technically. There was no user resistance. But the net result was that maintenance costs rose, production performance deteriorated and there were serious accidents. With the new formal procedures, the prime means of communication between production and maintenance operations was report forms. Production supervisors had to indicate on these forms the nature and gravity of breakdowns and then send the form to maintenance staff. This disrupted the previous close co-operation and interaction between skilled operators and supervisors, which helped anticipate symptoms of breakdowns and gather valuable information on maintenance.

* A large retail chain selling a variety of household goods, clothing, food and other commodities installed a centralized computer-based system to plan purchases for individual stores. The result was that the mix of items within stores became unbalanced and overall sales decreased. Previously, shop assistants provided information on which goods should be ordered. The new computer system disregarded shop employees' 'local memories' and defined replenishment policies purely on the basis of programmed procedures on the central system. The management system was therefore degraded and employees and customers were made unhappy.

* An engineering company introduced a computer system based on the PERT method to assist in project management. The system prepared a PERT diagram which identified all the key scheduled events and how they should be phased to ensure that the overall work was adequately integrated. A PERT diagram was prepared at the start of each project at the client's request. According to one engineer at the company, 'The project manager put the PERT diagram on the wall behind him, like a picture, and then watched it turn yellow'. The problem was that each change in the plan set up a chain of consequences and interactions that were too complex to be adequately catered for by the computer system. The costly computer system was therefore underutilized and most of the investment

was wasted. A completely different method of project management had to be introduced.

TYPES OF OFFICE TECHNOLOGY APPLICATIONS

New office technology is versatile. The same equipment can be programmed to carry out a variety of diverse functions. A word processor, for example, will have different effects depending on the environment in which it operates — whether it is in the office of a top executive or a typing pool; operating on its own or linked to a communications network; used in an office which receives information continuously or intermittently; and so on. The uses of office technology cannot therefore be identified by a simple list, with the name of the equipment on one side and its associated application on the other.

A more realistic and useful way of categorizing the applications of new office technology is summarized in Figure 6.1. This has four groups which are discussed in the following sections: mechanization; office information systems; computer aids; and decision support systems. Recognition that there are various groups and categories of office automation is an important aid in developing appropriate information systems that match the evolving needs of organizations.

Mechanization of office work

Implementing new office technology often starts with activities such as typing, electronic mail, filing and information retrieval. These can mechanize and replace human activities which form part or the whole of particular jobs. This type of office automation is introduced to improve 'productivity' by reducing staffing levels, improving speeds of information handling and generally cutting costs. Mechanization applications have often been associated with a piecemeal introduction of isolated and low cost equipment rather than being viewed as part of a complete system.

When mechanization has been the dominant or only form of office automation, the results have generally been poor, although they may have met limited performance and technical goals. Mechanization tends to lead to negative aspects highlighted in many examples in this book (such as in Chapter 7) — user resistance, often an overall increase in costs and decrease in efficiency (or at least gains that do not meet expectation), a high turnover of staff and a degradation in overall service. The reason is that the system has not been placed in the

Mechanization	Computer Aids
Examples: word processors, facsimile, teletext, microfilm, enhanced telephony, printers, phototypesetting	*Examples* electronic mail, viewdata, multifunction workstation, information storage and retrieval
Main relevant disciplines: ergonomics conventional work study, personnel management training	*Main relevant disciplines:* psychology, behavioural sciences, linguistics, human factors engineering, communications theory, artificial intelligence
Organization elements affected: tasks, jobs, formal organization structures, formal communication, conditions of employment, skills and qualifications	*Organization elements affected:* tasks, career development, training, job roles, communications (mainly for managers and professionals)
Main performance factors affected: clerical and secretarial productivity, staff turnover, absenteeism, staff motivation, product quality	*Main performance factors affected:* productivity and effectiveness of managers and professionals, product quality

Office information systems	Decision support systems
Examples: automation of office procedures, order recording, accounting, integration of data and text processing	*Examples:* financial planning models, portfolio management systems, simulation models, project developments
Main relevant disciplines: business and procedural analysis, operational research, management science, information analysis	*Main relevant disciplines:* decision sciences, cognitive psychology, management science, information requirements analysis
Organization elements affected: control and co-ordination procedures, job roles, boundaries between activities and units	*Organization elements affected:* as for office information systems, with an emphasis on the decision-making process
Main performance factors affected: the effectiveness and efficiency of units, systems flexibility and readiness to respond and adapt to changing needs	*Main performance factors affected:* productivity of managers and professional staff and of the groups and units as a whole

Figure 6.1: Types and impact of new office technology.

appropriate broader socio-technical context. The main initial impact of office mechanization has been on secretarial and clerical staff.

Computer-based office information systems

Many new office applications are often implemented as part, or an extension, of a data processing system and have the same risks and problems as those experienced in data processing. The prime aim of this type of system is to improve control, co-ordination and administrative functions. One of the main dangers is that the design and implementation have tended to focus on applications involving formal information structures and routine procedures. Office work, however, needs to be much more flexible, adaptable and ready to respond to unexpected events. The risk is increased because many of the tasks that are automated are extracted from more complete job functions, roles and organizational units. This can seriously damage the effectiveness of these roles and units.

Computer aids to office work

A variety of devices, systems and services provide tools to aid managers, professionals and other staff to carry out work. A multifunction workstation, for example, could provide: electronic mail capabilities; software to perform calculations, financial planning and many other information managing and processing tasks; information retrieval; and electronic filing of personal information. Many organizational and job aspects can be radically altered through the use of computer aids. For example, when electronic mail is used by a professional group developing and managing a complex project, their work processes and interactions may be redesigned because of the nature of electronic mail. The speed of communication and the ability for many people to interact via 'written' (electronic mail messages) communications provides new opportunities for quicker information exchange. This could radically alter working procedures and may also impose new constraints. If most communications are stored and logged in the computer system, individuals may be more cautious about suggesting innovative or risky ideas; informal 'off-the-record' communications methods may then develop.

Computer aids could therefore change:

— the tasks performed by professional, management, secretarial and clerical staff;

— the 'boundaries' between different job roles and the interaction between roles;

—the nature of communication;

—the way of designing work.

Decision Support Systems
Decision Support Systems help people to make decisions rather than automating the decision-making process itself. They enable the user to ask 'What if?' questions to see the different results that may be produced if various factors are altered. For example, a financial planning system could suggest what might happen if there are various inflation or interest rates. These systems can be of great benefit provided the user understands the limitations of the tech- niques involved (see Chapter 1) and the system is associated with appropriate management science, operations research and other techniques.

WHAT IS AN OFFICE?

Concepts of what exactly constitutes an office vary considerably. For some, offices are *places*. To others, they are amalgams of various *functions*. The idea of an office as a place is probably the most generally held view. 'I am going to the office', is the way someone describes going to the work place where office functions are carried out.

We prefer to view the office as a series of functions around which are created organization units, information systems, physical places and groupings of people. New office technologies provide new options regarding the physical location of these office functions. To view offices as places is an out-dated view which fails to give sufficient priority to important organizational aspects.

Taking this functional approach, two main types of offices can be identified:

— *Main process* offices which perform a primary task, such as insurance contract preparation, invoicing or handling personnel payroll payments.

— *Control and co-ordination* offices which are concerned mainly with managing various organizational units and carry out functions like planning and cost accounting. This type of office may be formalized into a special unit or its functions could be carried out in various units.

The impact of new office technology and the optimal organization of work will differ greatly in the two types of offices. The socio-technical approach provides analytical tools and principles which enable technology to be matched to an appropriate social environment (see Chapter 4). We would like to examine three aspects of such a design:

— *co-existing organizational layers:* the important idea that an organization unit should be viewed as a number of layers, each with a fresh perspective of the system;

— *the organization unit in motion:* how the office operates in practice;

— *configuration and structure of the unit:* the key organizational elements to be designed, their interdependence and expected performances.

TYPES OF ORGANIZATION WITHIN AN OFFICE

The contrast between a formal 'paper' organization and the informal 'real world' manner in which people behave within the organization is a major cause of difficulty in the planning and design of systems. We believe that there are a number of distinct 'organization' layers which coexist within an office; by 'organization' we mean a way of bringing together dispersed actions to meet common goals. These layers are shown in Figure 6.2; the precise definition of their numbers and types is less important than the realization that an office consists of more than just a single formal organizational structure. Other writers have different definitions than ours for terms like informal and *de facto* organization.

Each of the layers identified in Figure 6.2 has its own internal coherence, negotiation procedures, recognized authorities, and disciplines involved in their design and operation. Most attention has been given to the formal and informal layers by sociologists because these levels are of particular importance in manufacturing industry, which was the focus for most socio-technical design until the 1970s. The other layers are of more importance in service industries and white collar office work. All the layers must be integrated into an *overall organization* design. In the description and design of organizations, the following concepts are frequently referred to:

— *organizational unit:* the basic organizational structure;

—*boundaries:* the unit is regarded as carrying out a process surrounded by a boundary or interface with other units in the organization or with the 'outside' world;

—*open system:* an organization unit which has transactions beyond its boundaries, taking in various inputs and applying appropriate technology and work procedures to produce a variety of outputs from the unit.

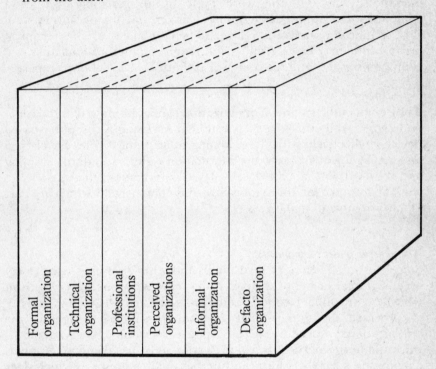

Figure 6.2   Layers of an organization

Formal organization

The formal organization is the system of written rules which regulate the actions of the members of the office. These include job descriptions, organizational charts, official procedures and standards. This layer is the most familiar one to anyone who has worked in an office. It provides a coherent 'system of government', controlled by management authority, missions and regulations which are in force within the boundaries of the organization. The formal organization is the one which usually dominates the technically-oriented approach to computer systems design. Although the formal layer is well known and easily recognized, it is not the most important one. In most offices, the formal organization regulates less than 20 per cent of its members' actions.

Technical procedures and methods

Many human actions and relationships at work are regulated by procedures which give directions for running equipment or technical operations, such as the work cycle in an assembly line or a computer-based information service. Custom and practice form part of this technical organization layer. The boundary of the technical organization may be external (say through communications links in a computer service) and the source of authority is the technical expert.

The design of the technical organization cannot be viewed in isolation. A designer who creates an environment for using a computer-based device is effectively providing, among other things: rules for clerical and management access to the information system; standards for filing and retrieval; formats for the display of information; the sequence of work operations; job roles; job skills; and other aspects which are part of other organizational layers.

Allegiance to wider communities

Some office staff belong to institutions and other groupings which form organizational layers of their own that extend through every unit in which their members work. In some units, the main regulatory activity is provided by professional institutions. When designing the organizational procedures for a hospital, for example, the regulations, rules and norms of the medical profession must be taken into account. Computing specialists form an international community which does not have the status of a formalized professional institution but which provides a strong influence in terms of promoting technical goals, establishing standards and evaluating achievements. The current technical trends within the computer profession can provide a strong pull towards more advanced technology rather than encouraging applications of proven and less exciting technology to meet organizational and user requirements.

How the organization is perceived

Individual members within an office perceive and interpret organizational regulations and rules in different ways. For example, authoritarian managers might regard strict control regulations as a vital ingredient in their power and authority; more open-minded managers might perceive rules as applying only to extreme cases when they are unable to get work done in other ways. Some clerks may regard formal rules as a natural and desirable part of the work environment; other clerks may see them as traps to be avoided.

The perceptions and expectations of individuals and subgroups have an important bearing on the behaviour of people in the office. Technology can cause significant changes in job roles and the way in which people regard office work. The subjective, qualitative judgements and views of those who work in the office should therefore be understood and catered for in developing office information systems.

Unplanned informal office activity

We refer to the 'informal organization' in a more restricted sense than many other writers, who regard the informal organization as covering all activities not defined in the formal organization. To us, it is the unplanned and unrecognized organization whose norms, goals, membership and leadership are different from those of the formal one. Work cliques and generation groups are examples of informal organizations. Unions, staff associations and sports clubs, however, are part of the institutional or formal setting. Informal organization can play a powerful role in determining how offices function. If they are strong enough, they can divert office procedures and facilities towards meeting the goals of the informal organization rather than the explicit aims of the office. The informal goals may, for example, be to increase the influence and power of the group, to provide individuals with more free time or to give the group an economic advantage over others.

The actual or de facto organization

The *de facto* organization is the set of unwritten rules and modes of action which are actually used to get work done but which are poorly understood and specified in the formal organization design. A secretary, for example, might have a *de facto* method of filing which is fast and efficient but which the manager cannot use because it has not been expressed in formal terms.

De facto methods are also needed in any managerial operations which require quick adaptations to meet situations unforeseen in formal organization procedures. Brian Wynne describes some *de facto* managerial methods in Chapter 8. In some cases, the *de facto* organization works very efficiently although it incorporates different concepts and principles to the other layers. This we call the *real organization*, which could be examined and used as the basis for redesigning the entire unit.

ADAPTING OFFICE PROCESSES

People in offices usually interact with the outside world in addition to carrying out completely internal operations. By considering a dynamic model of the 'office in motion', it becomes possible to achieve maximum adaptability to change in the external environment and to variations from the formal patterns of behaviour within the office. This avoids the danger of considering only the static, formal view of an organization.

Various processes carried out in the office have sometimes smaller, sometimes larger boundaries than the office's formal boundaries. The interactions with the external environment and internal uncertainties create disturbances, which cause changes *(variances)* from the ideal functioning of the unit as defined in the organization design. When such variances occur, people in the office must adapt quickly to the new needs, often by creating non-formal organizational structures. These can be diagnosed and then incorporated into the design in a similar way to the analysis of *de facto* organizations. Most failures in the introduction of computer-based systems are due to the variances from a design which was made to meet ideal processes defined on the basis of abstract technical or managerial expectations. This is exacerbated by the fact that most office work has a higher level of uncertainty than traditional data processing.

The main impacts of new office technologies on how the office operates in practice are likely to be:

— conversion work will decrease, i.e. tasks concerned with translating information from one form to another, such as receiving an order by telephone, writing it down, preparing required documentation and transmitting it to relevant departments, etc: all this could be done automatically by a computer-based system;

— co-ordination processes will become more complex because there will be an increase in the variety and capabilities of communications media;

— maintenance of procedures, know-how, standards and software will become a major part of office work;

— innovation in technology and procedures will take place more rapidly.

ANALYSIS OF OFFICE ORGANIZATION DESIGN

When designing an organizational unit, three inter-related aspects need to be considered — performance required, the structure of the unit and the 'configuration' which specifies the nature of the work in the unit.

Producing the required performance
Indicators must be provided of the type of performance sought and how it can be measured. These should include economic, technical and social criteria (see Chapter 2). Variances from the expected performance can be monitored to help determine whether and where changes need to be made.

Care must be taken to ensure that performance criteria take a broad view of requirements. A simple increase in the productivity of one part of the work-force carrying out a certain task, such as the typing activity of secretaries, does not necessarily mean there will be an overall improvement in the work of the office as a whole. Social criteria regarding the quality of working life also need to be included. They help to develop a healthy social environment and possibilities for individual growth as well as creating a climate conducive to more efficient and effective work practices.

The structure of the office
When introducing new technology into an existing office or starting up a new office, questions need to be asked about factors which influence the basic structure of the office, such as: the location, size and legal identification of the office; physical buildings, layout and equipment; characteristics and availability of staff — number, young/old, skilled/unskilled, and so on.

The way an office develops depends considerably on the environment in which the office exists, physically and socially. For example, changes in property prices in city centres and in transport costs could encourage a dispersal of the office population to regional areas and to the home, whereas incentives to revive inner-city areas may encourage a reverse trend. Changes in the composition and mobility of the labour market restrict the kinds of office organization which may be most effective in a particular area.

The creation of a suitable office structure requires careful evaluation and negotiation, involving managers from the organization, central and local public authorities, unions, architects, office building developers and others. These various disciplines and interests need to be recognized and incorporated in a careful socio-technical design programme.

The basic elements of organization design
Organization design must be broken down into specific components. The following are what we believe are the seven main elements of an organization.

— *Necessary aggregate work.* This is the amount and general quality of work needed. It is affected considerably by new office technologies and is often the main — or sole — criterion used by purchasers of new equipment.

— *Control systems and co-ordination procedures.* Some control procedures can be programmed into computer-based technology, which could reduce discretionary control from managers and the autonomy of self-regulated units. The formal organization can become dependent on these inbuilt control mechanisms.

— *Task structure.* This defines the contents of work tasks and the relationships between tasks. Tasks are often changed by new office technologies. The software of a word processor, for examples, determines the nature of the typing task. Task definitions in the formal organization can become subservient to the nature of the technology.

— *Formal organization.* As has already been discussed, this covers the formal definition of organization structure, jobs, internal procedures, communications channels and so on.

— *Job design.* New office technology may eliminate some clerical jobs and radically alter others (see Chapter 7). The assignment of tasks to individual jobs or job roles will also be influenced by new technologies. The availability of increased communications capabilities will change patterns of work and group interactions. Different forms of management control and management roles will also emerge (see Chapter 8). Roles combining varied tasks and interactions may substitute for the idea of individual jobs defined according to prescribed tasks.

— *Conditions of employment.* This covers aspects of the formal organization associated with labour relations and personnel department negotiations, such as wages and salaries, job qualifications, training, career development and working hours. Office technology could lead to many basic changes in the conditions of employment, including the possibility of more home-based office work.

—*Social organization*. This includes aspects of individual and group behaviour. For example, if a computer-based system severs the direct relationship between clerks and supervisors, social contact and co-operation could be adversely affected. On the other hand, the use of multifunction workstations in a network offers positive opportunities for completely new ways of co-operative work and individual and group interactions.

TECHNIQUES AND PRINCIPLES FOR OFFICE SYSTEMS DESIGN

Office systems have some general characteristics, such as:

—*uncertainty* of the nature of information received from and output to the external environment;

—*partly unspecified* processes and procedures which need to be adapted quickly to changing needs;

—*unstructured information* compared to traditional data processing tasks;

—*non-formal organizational layers* of greater importance than in a production process;

—*varied work force* with widely differentiated expectations and skills;

—*co-ordination and decision making* as key functions in many offices.

These kinds of system characteristics are particularly suited to the application of socio-technical methodologies. The socio-technical approach stresses that each organization and each office is unique and concentrates on investigating and describing actual events and relationships among different components rather than emphasizing quantified and formal aspects. The variety in information, work and people is taken into account by careful diagnosis and goal setting, which involves contributions from all aspects of office organization and people.

The need for a gradual evolution to new computer-based procedures is aided by the phased approach of socio-technical design, with an acceptance that the design should be adapted and changed during implementation to meet real world requirements. The process of diagnosis, design and implementation should be regarded as a continuous cycle rather than as a once-off exercise. As part of the design, a temporary organization might need to be established with, for example, a top-level *steering committee* to co-ordinate the process and executive control in the hands of a top manager who has been given a strong mandate (see Chapter 3).

It is not possible to suggest a single optimal model for the organizational design to be associated with new technology because each office has unique requirements and characteristics. The essence of the socio-technical approach is not to prejudge the design outcome or to try to apply standard solutions but to develop the most appropriate solution for each case.

RECOMMENDATIONS

1 Ensure that the design process is:

   — interdisciplinary, with representatives from all relevant areas and disciplines;

   — sensitive to the need to consider the multiple layers of organization that co-exist within an office;

   — planned but flexible;

   — negotiated among all those concerned.

2 Avoid a narrow focus on formal organization design and on aspects of new technology which automate and mechanize work, although these aspects do fit into a broader framework.

3 Regard the following design phases as a continuous process of evolution with considerable interaction between phases:

   — set goals;

   — prepare overall diagnosis;

— establish temporary organization with appropriate mandate and authority;

— decide approach to user participation;

— carry out analysis of system requirements

— make more detailed diagnoses and decisions as required which may differ from earlier ideas;

— prepare general overall 'architectural' framework design;

— develop and implement necessary training programmes;

— produce more detailed analytical designs;

— implement the system;

— evaluate the 'office in action' and alter the system accordingly.

4 Consider the following principles as a guide to designing organizations and jobs :

— *self-regulated organizational units* that allow the office to run a meaningful process with a visible result and that have an intrinsic readiness to adapt to changing requirements;

— *more flexible boundaries of units* where the same unit may encompass different processes or the same process is included in different units (say in an information network); this could mean that hierarchical management structures become less effective as co-ordination tools and that matrix and network forms of management are found to be more relevant;

— *minimal critical specification* of tasks with non-binding procedures to ensure maximum adaptability of work methods;

— *roles as the basic building blocks* of organizations rather than individual jobs; roles encompass a wider range of expectations, relationships and activities than jobs;

— *contents of roles* should emphasize key office tasks such as the control of variances from formal routines, co-ordination functions, and the maintenance and innovation of office routines, expertise and technology;

— *threats to physical and psychological well-being* removed and stress minimized;

— *work rotation* could be possible and desirable;

— *flexible working time and location* also becomes possible and desirable;

— *occupations* as a career progression with a succession of roles, evolving skills, continuous growth and visible rewards.

5 Ensure that the design matches real needs and that the design process is concerned with the description and analysis of actual events and relationships.

BIBLIOGRAPHY

Recommended reading of relevance to the issues discussed in this chapter include:

1 Argyris, C., 'Organizational Learning and Management Information Systems', *Accounting, Organisations and Society,* Vol 2, No 2, 1977.

2 Butera, F., 'Impact of New Technology on Work Organization in Production' in Beckermans, L. (ed.) *European Employment and Technological Change: A Seminar Sponsored by the EEC,* ECWS, Maastricht, Holland 1982.

3 Crozier, M., Friedberg, E., *L'acteur et le sytème,* Editions du Seuil, Paris, 1977.

4 Davis, L.E., 'Optimising Plant and Organisation Design', *Organisation Dynamics,* Autumn, 1979.

5 De Maio, A., Bartezzaghi, E., and Zanarini, G., 'A New System Analysis Method Based on the STS Approach' in Schneider H. J. (ed.), *Formal Models and Practical Tools for Information Systems Design,* North-Holland, Amsterdam, 1972.

6 Driscoll, J.W., *Office Automation: the Organizational Redesign of Office Work*, Centre for Information Systems Research, MIT, Sloan School of Management, Cambridge, MASS, 1979.

7 Keen, P.G.W., Scott Morton, M.S., *Decision Support Systems: an Organizational Perspective*, Addison-Wesley, Reading, MASS, 1978.

8 Zisman, M.D., 'Office Automation: Revolution or Evolution', *Sloan Management Review*, Spring, 1978.

CHAPTER 7: THE CHANGING ROLES OF SECRETARIES AND CLERKS

Niels Bjørn-Andersen

INTRODUCTION

There are two widely different views of the nature of the 'office of the future'. The technologist's *dream* is of a spacious and well-lit room filled with sleek modern office equipment and cool, smiling managers and secretaries. Computer-based technology performs all the routine tasks, leaving people with challenging and creative jobs aided by the availability of accurate and timely information at their fingertips. The sociologist's *nightmare* is that the 'factory has taken over the office'[1]. In the nightmare, all office functions have been automated. Exploited and deskilled employees input information to the computer and fill in the gaps between automated processes. Work is highly structured and preprogrammed, and piece-work rates and machine-pacing are used to control office workers.

This chapter identifies the likely *actual* changes in offices due to new information technologies. Staff reactions to these developments are discussed. An important part of the chapter is a description of the factors which could make the 'ideal' new office jobs. There is also a discussion of how to handle the transition to the new electronic office.

NEW JOB PATTERNS

New office technology, as explained by André Danzin in Chapter 1, will lead to a convergence of data, text and voice processing through integrated communications networks. This will create a situation where many — though by no means all — office functions are supported or carried out using computer-based methods. Typical functions which could be partly or fully automated include: the filing and retrieval of text and pictures; editing text reports and letters; the communication of messages and other information; production of printed material; and computations of every kind.

The increased use of these capabilities will gradually alter the nature of office work. It will also have an impact on levels of employment. New technology will be substituted for human labour in many activities where it is economically desirable and feasible. On the other hand, the technology will generate new goods and services and will help to maintain and improve the competitiveness of individual companies and countries, thereby creating new jobs.

It is difficult, however, to put precise numbers on these changes, particularly as circumstances will vary considerably in different countries and regions and between different sectors of the workforce, such as between men and women, the young and the old, the skilled and the unskilled (see also Chapter 9). In periods of economic constraint the emphasis in introducing new technology will often be based on 'machines for people' cost arguments, which lead to justified fears amongst existing employees that the prime management aim of implementing new technology is to cut staffing levels, thereby creating opposition to technological change.

CHANGES IN OFFICE WORK DUE TO NEW TECHNOLOGY

There are some deterministic features of new office technology — changes which will almost always occur when the technology is introduced. This should not be taken to mean that there will be a uniform set of changes in response to technological innovation in the office. Different consequences for work methods, people and organizations will result from different techniques of designing and implementing the new systems. Three of the main deterministic effects on office work relate to skills, formalization of office work, and polarization of jobs.

Clerical and secretarial skills
Clerks and secretaries will perform fewer specific tasks directly but will be expected to spend more time on monitoring or supervizing processes carried out by computer-based devices. Instead of possessing the basic skills (like calculating a result, preparing statistics, typing and laying out a letter or spelling words), they will have to learn how to operate the automatic system. Thus, the ability to evaluate and exploit the capabilities of computer systems will become a key qualification for office jobs. New technology will cause significant changes in education and training (see Chapter 12). The EEC Centre for Vocational Training[2], has found that the skills needed to work with microelectronics-based production equipment meant that the training time for new operators

was lower than with the old system. The same could happen with computer-based office work.

Formalization and structure in office work

In a study I helped carry out into the impact of five very different types of computer systems in banks in four countries[3], for most of the factors analyzed, there was no clear unified direction of impact. The only aspect where there was a consistent and unambiguous direction of change was that the degree of structure, preprogramming and formalization required by computer systems meant that there was a reduction in the choice available to the individual employee. Predefined codes, programmed procedures and other structural rules are necessary to reap the benefits of computers. This will still be true even though computer systems are becoming more flexible and adaptable to individual requirements.

Polarization in jobs

Taylorism (see Chapter 4) has been one of the most potent philosophies based on the principle of the division of labour. On the assembly line, it created a large number of very routine, low skilled jobs for workers, with the more skilled and challenging tasks moved to specialized departments. At the same time, of course, it brought a high degree of material prosperity to many in industrialized countries.

This tendency to create a polarization in job content, skills level and salary between the worker operating a machine and staff planning the system has often been repeated with computer-based office systems. Users are frequently unaware of some of the simplest aspects of a system which has been designed by highly qualified specialist departments. When I visited an office stationery wholesaler, for example, a clerk told me that there were three keys on her keyboard she was not allowed to touch. She did not know what would happen if she did so.

Office work generally has a woolly, changing and informal character which, to a large extent, relies on the adaptive skill of the staff to cope with new situations. If office routines require limited skills and are tightly specified, the system could become too rigid and staff could lose the ability to handle the non-standard or non-programmed tasks which constantly arise in offices. Highly structured jobs with a low skill content are also those which are most easily eliminated through automation. The polarization of office work could therefore lead to the complete replacement of many secretarial and clerical jobs by programmed computers.

Changing relationships between managers and secretaries

The polarization of office work will also have an impact on the traditional secretarial role, as well as on clerical functions. This, in turn, will change management roles and the interactions between managers and secretaries.

Typing usually amounts to only about 15-30 per cent of the total work done by secretaries, although they usually feel that they spend more time on typing tasks. Part of this time can be saved by the use of word processing. The new capabilities will also lead to a lessening of the workload placed on secretaries because systems will be used directly by managers, supervisors, professional people, scientists, senior clerks and others. The traditional secretarial role is therefore being reduced. The result will be a cut in the number of secretaries and/or the creation of new secretarial roles, of which I can identify three possibilities, the *office-wife, Girl-Friday* or *co-worker* role.

The removal of routine tasks by office technology could mean that secretaries revert to a traditional role that can be characterized as an 'office-wife', providing general support to the manager, passing on relevant gossip, and generally fulfilling the tasks traditionally carried out by a private secretary. Although there may be an increase in this type of personal service to some managerial positions, changing social attitudes and the elimination of the legitimacy of using a secretary as a status symbol means that the office-wife role is unlikely to grow significantly.

It is more likely that the secretary will gradually take over a Girl-Friday role — subordinate to an authoritarian boss but taking on some practical responsibilities, such as information retrieval, telephoning and other activities previously carried out by personal assistants or higher-graded clerks. This upgrading and enlargement of the secretary's job could take over some of the more structured parts of a manager's job.

In contrast to the authoritarian approach implicit in the Girl-Friday relationship, the secretary could become a genuine partner or colleague to the manager. This could mean that new office technology could be used to provide the opportunity for new divisions of labour in the office. These new roles could be built on job rotation, job enrichment and job sharing according to the interests or special qualifications of employees rather than by predefined formal positions. At the Copenhagen Business School, for example, some secretaries have taken on responsibilities for tasks like the administration of students' studies, negotiations with publishers over research papers, popularizing research projects and teaching. Equally, professional lecturers have started doing some secretarial tasks, like writing letters part of their time.

The kind of new technology selected can have a decisive influence in limiting or expanding job roles. If a secretary were provided with a stand-alone word processor, for example, she would be unable to carry out those tasks which would be part of an enlarged and more creative role. This would require access to systems with comparable capabilities to an executive workstation, such as communications and information retrieval.

Carrying out office work at home
The communications capabilities of new office technology provides the potential to distribute office work away from central office sites to neighbourhood centres or to the homes of individual employees. The extent to which this will occur will be determined by sociological aspects — there are no major technological difficulties.

For the organization, the dispersal of work has obvious advantages, such as a reduction in the need for office accommodation. Highly skilled managers or professionals are likely to view the possibility of working from home as an advantage because they will have a choice of whether or not to work from a terminal or go into the office. This choice will be perceived as a luxury, particularly as the tasks being performed from home are likely to be relatively creative.

For a less skilled, typically female, clerk the prospect of working from home may be less attractive. An important reason for working from home for this type of staff would be to look after children while earning a living. Working at a terminal, however, is likely to require a high degree of accuracy and concentration which makes it incompatible with looking after a child. The ergonomic environment is also likely to be unsatisfactory.

The type of work that can be devolved to the home will involve activities which require little interaction with colleagues and a minimum of work instruction. Studies of job satisfaction, however, indicate that social contact is one of the most frequently cited reasons for going to work. Professionals and managers will be compensated for the lack of human contact because they will have a choice about whether to and when to do their creative work at home. For typists and clerks, home work is likely to consist of routinized and structured tasks, such as power typing at a word processor. They are also likely to work under the pressure of piece-work payments and with detailed controls over their work performance. Being deprived of contact with adults while performing routine tasks could lead to a great deal of stress and feelings of alienation.

The neighbourhood 'technological office centre' offers a form of more distributed work which maintains social contacts. The centre would be equipped with advanced office and communications systems which can be used by staff working for different employees. These will be sited closer to the employees than city centre office blocks.

STAFF RESPONSES TO TECHNOLOGICAL CHANGE

Management regards 'overcoming resistance to change' as an important stage in paving the way to technological change. The response to change, however, covers many different actions, from enthusiastic acceptance to violent resistance. The means of overcoming any resistance also vary from a positive and co-operative approach by managers and staff to deceptive manipulation by a distrustful and authoritarian management. Figure 7.1 which I have developed from a classification

Type of response	Staff reactions
Acceptance	— enthusiastically co-operate and support — co-operate — co-operate under pressure from management — accept with reluctance
Indifference	— passively resign to 'fate' — indifference/apathy — lose interest in work — avoid learning
Active resistance	— reduce work activity level to a minimum — protest — work-to-rule and go-slow — make deliberate mistakes — destroy 'by accident' — sabotage

Figure 7.1 Possible staff reactions to technological innovation.

originated by Arnold Judson[4], indicates the main ways in which staff of all levels could respond to technological change:

— employees perceive a *negative overall result* of the change, such as possible redundancies, reduced social contacts at work or less autonomy within the job role;

— employees are *uncertain about the consequences,* knowing what they have already got and fearful of future unknowns;

— the employer's desire to introduce new technology is seen by employees as a *lever to increase their bargaining power* during negotiations covering broader labour relations issues.

The third of these factors can be handled during the process of negotiating technological change, as discussed by John Evans in Chapter 9. Other reasons for resistance to change could be handled by:

— *compensation,* such as through redundancy payments or extra money for operators of new equipment;

— *humanizing the design* of the system and aiming to minimize layoffs;

— *user participation* in systems development;

— *providing users with adequate information, education and training,* including pilot tests to give experience before the full system is installed.

Compensation and humanization are legitimate means of trying to overcome fears that new systems will be detrimental to employees. Positive attitudes can also be encouraged by showing that, after the technology is introduced, the employee's position will be relatively better than the previous situation.

If the main reason for resistance is uncertainty about long-term consequences, the fear could be overcome by user participation and the provision of appropriate information, education and training. Users will feel they have some chance of influencing the future of their own working environment and will be in a position to judge the likely benefits for themselves. These solutions are not a universal panacea. If the system is going to lead to some job losses, negotiated redundancy payments are the only real way of placating staff who will indeed suffer.

In order to allay fears about the unknown consequences of change, positive attitudes are more easily obtained if it can be shown that the new systems will be simple to understand and use. Staff should also be given an opportunity of testing what the consequences might be before the system is completed.

These policies for creating positive staff attitudes have been criticized by some unions and staff as being 'manipulative' management devices, which mask the underlying disadvantages for staff. If the situation gets into a stalemate due to wider labour relations and political considerations, all management strategies will probably be viewed as manipulative. The problems can then be resolved only through negotiation. However, I would strongly urge management to avoid the temptation to indulge in deliberate manipulation to hide unpalatable facts. This would be hard to justify on moral grounds and could eventually create a distrust in management which will encourage active resistance to new technology.

IDEAL REQUIREMENTS FOR FUTURE OFFICE JOBS

There is no such thing as a universal specification for an 'ideal job'. People have different expectations of what an ideal job would be, depending on their own backgrounds, attitudes, qualifications and experiences. An ideal job must start with a picture of the person to fill it and must be built to fit the particular individual and organizational requirements.

For example, in the mid-1970s, I examined the jobs of clerks working in three banks[5]. Systems departments in the banks had introduced three types of computing service. The most technologically primitive was the batch system, where the users had no direct terminal link to a central computer. The most advanced was a 'real time' service, where the users could interact with the computer, receiving immediate responses. In between was the data entry system, which provided terminal links for entering data but not for other transactions. I measured the level of routine in the jobs of direct clerical users and *indirect users,* the clerks in the banks who were not operators of the computer service.

The results of the study showed that the job content of direct users got poorer and more routinized as the systems became more technologically advanced. Indirect users had a similar job content level with all systems. The clerks most satisfied with their jobs, however, were the direct users in the bank with the real-time computer service, although their jobs were the most routinized. The main reason for this was that these clerks were very low skilled women who had no broader banking expertise. Their new jobs in the banks were regarded as preferable to their previous jobs, such as sales staff in supermarkets.

There are four main factors which influence the design of jobs — job content, work autonomy, ergonomics and psychological aspects. Ergonomics and psychological requirements are discussed in Chapters 10 and 11. In the following sections of this chapter, I examine job content and work autonomy in more detail, but first I would like to emphasize a general requirement for flexibility in design. No two offices are alike. The same office changes over a period of time. The office systems designed today should therefore be flexible enough to cater for different ways of organizing the office in the future. Only in this way will it be possible to achieve efficiency and job satisfaction and avoid user resistance.

JOB CONTENT

There are many ways in which job content can be described but I have found that the best results are obtained when the criteria examined are kept to a manageable number. Three of the most important dimensions of job content are the degree of specialization, the amount of structure and preprogramming, and the extent to which decisions are taken according to pre-defined rules.

Specialization
The general tendency in office work has been towards increasing specialization. Clerks with general backgrounds capable of handling a large variety of tasks have gradually disappeared. The main reasons have been a growing complexity in office work at the same time as managers and organization/job designers have attempted to reduce education requirements for office jobs.

For example, although the prices of computer terminals and word processors have been falling, they can still be fairly expensive. As recently as 1981, a report from the Swedish government concluded, 'in a normal office environment, the use of word processors cannot be justified economically unless they can be utilized all day'[6]. This has led to strong pressures to make one or two clerks specialize in operating word processors.

Over-specialization has its price. It can lead to the creation of boring jobs with limited scope for learning and initiative on behalf of the staff. This frequently results in a loss of job satisfaction and, sometimes, the creation of operational inefficiency. For example, when I was studying the impact of computers on bank clerks, I was the only customer in a branch bank in a suburb of Copenhagen. As soon as I entered the door, a lamp flashed on the wall telling me to go to cashier 2. All three teller counters had a clerk. I asked her why she had lit her lamp instead of leaving me to choose from one of the three unoccupied tellers. She said that, when the clerks had nothing else to do, they played a game to see who was fastest to light her lamp when a customer came in. Specialization can therefore cause creativity and energy to be channelled into wasteful activities.

Provided the computer system has been designed with sufficient flexibility, most job functions can be enlarged to encompass a variety of activities and skills. In most cases, it would be advisable to let the clerks handle all matters in relation to a given customer/project, aided by appropriate computing and word processing support. Another possibility that has been found useful is to establish semi-autonomous work groups around one or two sets of modern office technology.[7]

Structuring and preprogramming

A clerk once commented to me that, 'with all the discussion about intelligent terminals, the computer specialists seem to forget that there is intelligence in front of the screen'. This pinpoints a key question to be resolved in applying information technology. Is the technology to be shaped into a tool which can be used by the well educated clerk or is it to be used to dictate detailed procedures and instructions which could be followed by a child?

The tendency in information technology has been to make the systems more and more self-contained, leaving less and less to the discretion of the operator. When I was shown a large real-time system by the head of a computer department, he proudly said, 'This system is absolutely fool-proof. Go on — you try it'. He was unaware of the implicit insult. Trying my best, I could do nothing but follow the prescribed procedures.

I accept that it is a justifiable design objective to make a system 'robust' so that operator errors cannot cause serious damage. I seriously question, however, whether people should be expected to carry out procedures day-in and day-out which have been designed for a 'fool'. Clerks carrying out such jobs will be unable to handle unexpected situations, say when the computer system breaks down. Furthermore, having worked in such an environment for many years, clerks will strongly resist any kind of change because they will rightly be uncertain about their own capability of handling the change.

Rule-oriented decisions

A typical bureaucratic problem is that decisions are often made on the basis of a large number of standard rules. A more adaptable approach to decision making is to consider the *consequences* of a given solution. With their potential for being programmed, computers are naturally biased towards reinforcing rule-oriented rather than consequence-oriented decision making. Advanced software can handle a vast number of criteria and rules of far greater complexity than any individual or organizational group can manage.

Computer systems should not be allowed to reinforce some of the most unresponsive aspects of bureaucracies by making it easier to apply more rules (see Chapter 5). If this happens, few users or clients will understand the reasoning behind the conclusion coming out of the system. When a client criticizes the bureaucracy, the bureaucracy will defend itself by pointing to a rule, creating a new rule or merely saying that 'computer decisions' cannot be over-ruled.

Computer systems should therefore be developed which assist staff to keep track of all activities relating to a particular function. Staff should be able to evaluate consequences of particular actions and should be capable of adapting the system to produce tailor-made solutions to fit the clients' requirements.

Summary on job content

These issues regarding job content can be summarized by the two diagrams in Figures 7.2. If it is assumed that staff have little systems competence in knowing about the technology and business (top left-hand corner of Figure 7.2a) then a negative spiral is set up, ending with little job satisfaction and high staff turnover. On the other hand, if systems are designed assuming a high standard of systems competence, a positive spiral is created (Figure 7.2b).

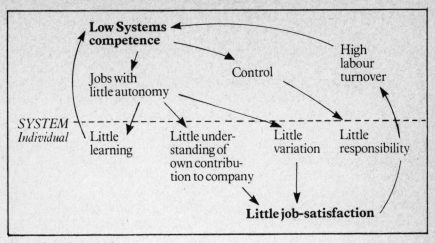

(a)   Negative spiral

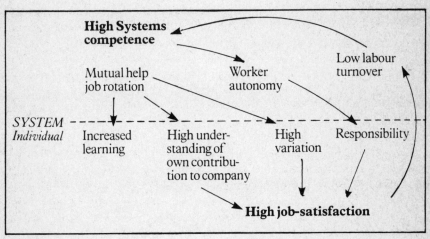

(b)   Positive spiral

Figure 7.2   Impact of different approaches to job content design

AUTONOMY AND CONTROL

Information technology provides the basis for major changes in activities which influence the amount of autonomy and control exercised by individuals and groups within an organization. These changes include the amount of performance-monitoring undertaken and the degree of influence which an individual is allowed over their own work role.

Information systems can also have an impact on the effectiveness of industrial democracy which seeks to give all staff some say in influencing the way the organization develops. Various forms of industrial democracy have been implemented, such as through Works Councils (see Chapter 9). Whatever form is used, staff can get some of the benefits which are offered by the availability of a good computerized information service. In some companies, employees have established their own computer-based 'workers' information system'.

Control of work performance
Computer-based systems provide the technical possibility for second-to-second supervision of the operator. Many employee groups have objected to these facilities. In a French insurance company, for example, the clerks went on strike until management removed a personal identity plastic-card system which meant that all doors in the company could be opened only with the card — even the toilet door. In a Danish shipyard, the union threatened to go on strike if a planned new production control system was linked to an existing computerized personnel information system. This would have made it possible to provide detailed reports on work performance. The management withdrew the proposal after the strike threat.

In many organizations, however, employees have accepted detailed accounts of their performance by computer monitoring. This has happened with jobs in supermarkets, data entry departments and some offices. In particular, young employees with career expectations and with no worry about meeting targets seem more ready to accept this kind of working environment.

Excessive and ill-planned monitoring, however, may be detrimental to individuals and to overall effectiveness. Firstly, employees may shift their energy and creativity away from the job itself into 'beating the system'. I know a long-haul lorry driver who told me that he and his friends had found eight ways of beating the device which monitors their driving — within a week of the device being made compulsory.

Secondly, detailed controls of a limited aspect of employee's performance will automatically lead to employees trying to meet only those
objectives that may be monitored while forgetting about other aspects
which are vital but unquantifiable, such as service, advice and help to
colleagues.

Puppets on a string?

Traditional office work has not allowed staff to have much influence on
the planning of work. The clerk is either controlled by a person or an
administrative procedure. In practice, though, the clerk may have a
considerable degree of autonomy in the overall work environment, such
as in the scope for choosing the sequence of work and even, to some
extent, freedom to use one's own methods and initiative.

Increased computerization has tended to reduce the autonomy of the
individual in order to achieve greater co-ordination and utilization of
resources. Tasks which were previously carried out *assisted* by a
computer have often been transferred completely to a computer-based
system. For example, the loan officer of a Danish bank said to me that a
new computer system allowed him to award a greater loan than he
could previously, as part of a move to 'decentralization' in the bank.
Instead of feeling liberated, he felt castrated. Although he could award
more money, he had been provided with detailed loan policy rules about
to whom, for what purpose and on what terms he could give a loan.
Furthermore, the computer system would immediately report to headquarters about any deviations from the rules.

There is no intrinsic technological reason why computers should be
used to reduce autonomy. Using the systems design approach described
in Chapters 4 and 6, modern office systems could be built to enhance
decentralized decision making by providing employees with better
information support, rather than reducing them to puppets on a string.

PSYCHOLOGICAL ASPECTS

One of the most important psychological requirements of any type of
worker is a sense of self-achievement. To satisfy this, the job should have
some challenges but should not exceed the capabilities of the person
doing it. Jobs created with computer-based systems could be too dull
and routine, which would lead to a sense of under-achievement or, at the
other extreme, they can increase stress levels (see Chapter 11).

Social contact and alienation

When new office technology is introduced, the amount of social contact and interaction between individuals is often reduced because there is more direct interaction between the user and the machine. Word processor operators have been placed in separate rooms because of the noise from printers; bank clerks and tellers have been isolated because the equipment takes up so much space that staff can talk to colleagues only by shouting; and many employees in ordinary office environments have been given such specialized job functions that there are few, if any, legitimate reasons for talking to colleagues.

Computers are also often perceived as mysterious and threatening and frequently lead to boring jobs after they have been introduced. This can emphasize feelings of alienation, which have already become widespread in modern industrialized society. If the computer system is complex and difficult to understand and use, the sense of alienation will be exacerbated.

A job environment with minimal social contact and high degree of alienation provides little job satisfaction and may threaten the overall effectiveness of the organization. Decisions may be supported by data computed to the nth decimal place but may nevertheless be wrong because an operator with no understanding or interest in the problem has formulated the input information incorrectly.

HOW TO HANDLE THE TRANSITION

Managing the transition to the 'office of the future' is not an easy task. The changes that will take place in secretarial and clerical roles could cause many groups to be sceptical about the consequences of automation. The most effective and acceptable way of overcoming staff resistance is to enable employees to take an active part in designing their own work environment. This participation is an important factor in the negotiation of technology agreements (see Chapter 9). Such participation, however, will fail to meet its objectives if users are provided with inadequate education (see Chapter 12).

Such education should be oriented towards enabling users to formulate requirements and to evaluate the benefit of proposed solutions in their particular working environment, producing significant improvements in the design of office systems. Too often, however, education and training of users are aimed merely at teaching employees to operate equipment that has already been selected without user involvement.

RECOMMENDATIONS

1   Establish mechanisms to consider and negotiate how to design and implement the secretarial and clerical job roles which result from the introduction of new office technology.

2   Avoid staff resistance by involving users in systems design to ensure that there is a sufficient 'fit' between the organizational, human and technical systems to make users perceive the new systems as technological aids not technological menaces.

3   Plan a labour relations strategy within a stable framework which prepares for any necessary changes in personnel policies, such as job design, education and training, rather than allowing problems to fester and explode when they reach a crisis point (see Chapter 9).

4   Provide flexible hardware and software and appropriate education to allow users to have the prime responsibility in developing and tailoring systems to their particular needs.

5   Develop guidelines on desirable characteristics of jobs. Dimensions which should be considered as the basis for job roles of clerks and secretaries include:

   — *formalization and specialization:* if jobs become over-formalized and over-specialized, many staff will no longer have the adaptive skills to cope with changing and unpredictable office work requirements;

   — *rule-oriented decision making:* the computer should not cause too many decisions to be made on the basis of pre-programmed rules instead of learning from the consequences of previous experiences;

   — *autonomy and control:* staff should have an influence in planning work methods and a degree of freedom in choosing how to carry out operational activities;

   — *work performance control:* the degree to which computers monitor and control work should not be excessive;

   — *stress:* there should be a sufficient level of job autonomy and absence of direct controls to avoid excessive stress (see Chapter 11);

   — *social contact and alienation:* computers should not be allowed to severely limit opportunities for social contact amongst staff.

6 Re-evaluate the relationship between managers and secretaries to take account of changing work roles and procedures.

7 Consider the social and human, as well as the economic, benefits and problems offered by the technological potential to perform office work from home.

REFERENCES

1 Hoos, I.R., 'When the Computer Takes Over the Office', *Harvard Business Review,* July-August, 1960.

2 Træsborg, M., Bjørn-Andersen, N., *Microelectronics and Work Qualifications,* Report to CEDEFOP (EEC Centre for Vocational Training), Copenhagen, 1981.

3 Bjørn-Andersen, N., Hedberg, B., Mercer, D., Mumford, E., Solé, A., *The Impact of Systems Change in Organizations,* Sijthoff & Nordhoff, Amsterdam, 1979.

4 Judson, A.S., *Styring af Ændringer i Virksomheden,* Copenhagen, 1972.

5 Bjørn-Andersen, N., 'Organizational Aspects of Systems Design', *Data,* no 12, 1976.

6 Statskonsult, *Erfarenhetsstudie ord-och Testbehandling,* Stockholm, 1981.

7 Mumford, E., Weir, M., *Computer Systems in Work Design — the ETHICS Method,* Associated Business Press, London, 1979.

BIBLIOGRAPHY

Recommended reading of relevance to the issues discussed in this chapter, in addition to the above references, include:

Bjørn-Andersen, N. (ed.), *The Human Side of Information Processing,* North-Holland, Amsterdam, 1980.

Borum, F. (ed.) *Edb, Arbejdsmiljø og Virksomhedsdemokrati,* Nyt fra Samfundsvidenskaberne, Copenhagen, 1977.

Galitz, W.O., *Human Factors in Office Automation*, Life Office Management Association, 1980.

Hansen, H.R., Schröder, K.T., Weohe, H.J., (eds.), *Mench und Computer*, Oldenburg Verlag, Munich, 1979.

Sandberg, Å., (ed.), *Computers Dividing Man and Work*, Arbetslivscentrum, Stockholm, 1979.

CHAPTER 8: THE CHANGING ROLES OF MANAGERS

Brian Wynne

INTRODUCTION

Changes in secretarial and clerical work have often been the focus of attention in general discussions on the effects of new office technology (see Chapter 7). The impact on managers, however, is of equal importance both in terms of costs and numbers. Secretarial and typing activities typically account for about 10 per cent of office labour costs compared to 60-75 per cent for managers and professional staff. From the mid-1970s, the numbers of managers and professional people grew at a faster rate than secretaries, typists and clerks. Management and professional levels now form the largest segment of office staff.[1] In addition, managers are key users of information and are likely to be the group most profoundly affected by attempts to automate information processes.

This chapter examines the diverse roles played by information in different management roles, emphasizing the crucial influence of *informal* information flows and organizational interactions in determining management effectiveness. Advice is provided on how to develop systems which are adapted to the actual way organizations and managers operate and which enlarge the scope and interest of management jobs.

THE IMPORTANCE OF INFORMATION TO MANAGEMENT ROLES

A defining feature of the management role is its relationship to information. Management performs creative actions on information whereas other staff usually relate passively to it. Many management actions involve some degree of shaping information by, say, interpreting data for a progress report or using information to help select between strategic options. Other staff who use a great deal of information, such as secretaries and clerks, tend to process it mechanically.

There have been many attempts to 'rationalize' management. The information technologies which comprise new office systems have provided a fresh impetus to these efforts. For example, one of the earliest office technology projects, at Citibank in the USA, was motivated by a finding that managers spent 60 per cent of their time on paperwork which could be eliminated by automation.

The potential for automating many management tasks has led to a gradual enlargement of ambition for applying computer-based systems to management activities. At first, the main applications were of individual technologies with little or no calculative capacity, such as electronic mail, aimed at reducing 'wasted' time. The individual technologies have subsequently been integrated to include routine management tasks involving some calculative but little creative content, such as monitoring budgets and receiving updated information on production progress. This led to what an experienced office system analyst, Jim Driscoll, called the 'technological boondoggle', which seeks to encompass the majority of management actions, including creative decision making.

The comprehensive 'boondoggle' approach to office information systems is likely to cause a radical revision of traditional management roles and a polarization within management on the degree to which the new systems increase or decrease the autonomy and power of the manager. In information-related definitions, 'top management' will make decisions which are unique and important and will be relatively unaffected by new technology. Many of the 'middle' management decisions could become dependent on computer-based processing, with a very small degree of freedom allowed for an individual's interpretation of the computerized results compared to a much higher degree of autonomy for similar middle management functions in the past (see the '*Puppets on a String?*' section in Chapter 7). Many previous managerial and supervisory roles could be almost completely automated, being turned into primarily clerical or machine-operation tasks.

AUTOMATED MANAGEMENT: THE REALITIES

The organizational context in which management works should influence the design of the information system. Many computer-based systems have been developed in isolation from their broader social interactions (see Chapter 2). There is a great deal of evidence available

about the way managers actually operate. This should be understood
and taken into account by new office technology planners and designers.

The informal management network

The most important aspects of organizational behaviour to be considered when designing information systems are the often unacknowledged,
hidden but highly influential, informal organizational structures (see
also Chapters 5 and 6). These have inbuilt patterns of information
channels, control and distribution which are different to those which are
meant to prevail officially. Yet it has often been the official routines that
have formed the basis of system specifications.

In one organization, it was found that a middle manager wielded great
influence over top management's decisions because he acted as a
'gatekeeper' in passing intelligence information between middle and top
management levels.[2] This power over information enabled him to
manipulate the information to ensure that judgements reflected his own
interests. His actual information power-base was far greater than that
recognized in the formal system. Personal relationships between managers at different levels in this organization were found to be of crucial
practical significance. The credibility of information emanating from
middle management was strongly determined by the degree to which
the top management knew and trusted the person who was its source.
The informal personal relations acted as an 'information bypass',
short-circuiting formal channels. This is typical of most organizations.

Powerful information systems can both increase the volume of information available to managers and remove the filtering device of trusted
relationships. This could lead to a reduction in the effectiveness of senior
decision makers. They can be overwhelmed by information without
having a reliable mechanism to distinguish between the pertinent and
the irrelevant, the reliable and the untrustworthy messages and data.

Middle management often has the power to conceal unpalatable facts
by the unofficial selection of information channelled to senior levels.
American management specialist Chris Argyris examined one organization in which top management was wholly dependent on middle
management for the selection and interpretation of information reaching
them.[3] Systematic distortions were taking place which reflected middle
management interests or conceptions of the organization's interest. On
one occasion, the poor performance of one sector was completely
concealed from top management until a severe crisis developed.

This danger can be the result of senior management's request to have key issues boiled down to 'a single sheet of paper'. The bias in selecting information may come from a desire by middle managers to present what they think senior management would like to hear, rather than from a deliberate conspiracy to hide the truth.

In these circumstances, middle management often shift the blame back to top management by pointing out that they had access to all the raw, unprocessed data. Theoretically, this is true, although in practice no senior manager would have the time to sift through all this basic information. It might therefore seem desirable to have the 'neutral' mechanism of a computer-based information system to avoid personal bias. This could, however, lead to many of its own problems.

Information system bias
People can obviously distort, suppress and manipulate information for their own purposes. Managers are generally aware of this potential for human bias and develop their own personal informal information and advice channels to cross-check and expand on information received. Computer-based systems, however, give the *appearance* of objectivity because they can provide quantified results that give the impression of great accuracy. In practice, these figures may be wrong, the information processing that produces them may ignore crucial factors, or they may be distorted by the assumptions built into the programs.

Information is often used to legitimize decisions already made. The apparent 'objectivity' of reports from computer-based systems makes them ideally suited to what Anthony Hopwood in Chapter 2 calls a 'rationalization machine' to justify decisions already made. The increased volume of information whose credibility and source are difficult to verify could conceal the real factors and interests involved, leading to bad decisions.

The experience of the Kansas City Police Department illustrates another way in which computer-based systems could cause bias in an organization. The Department installed a highly successful automated information system which assisted with traffic offences. After a time, however, it was found that too much attention and management effort was going into this relatively unimportant field, to the detriment of more serious crime. Other organizations have also found that the availability of an apparently precise information system can focus management attention on a relatively trivial area at the expense of more important management problems which can be less well defined in computing terms.

THREATS TO MANAGEMENT EFFECTIVENESS

Informal empire-building or systematic filtering of information to top management may be designed to further the interests of particular groups. It can also, however, be of benefit to the organization as a whole because it helps to adapt to changing real requirements which may be different from the formal goals perceived by top management. This ability to have some say in directly influencing the organizational environment is of vital importance to middle management's autonomy, accountability, power, status and motivation.

Chapters 5 and 6 showed how computer-based systems can enforce an increased 'transparency' of organizational procedures which makes explicit the formal view of management processes and examined the various levels that exist in organizations. The formal organizational level is the one most easily and most often computerized. New office technology could therefore result in a significant reduction in the informal flexibility which is so crucial to individual management roles as well as to the total organizational performance.

Loss of management autonomy
If the information system is based on the formal model of authority and information flows, or if it has been intentionally designed to force the organization to become 'more rational', it will fail to match real human and social needs. It could remove many of the traditional negotiating, bargaining and decision-making skills of middle management. This will cause a feeling of alienation by damaging or destroying the constructive functioning of the informal information networks and social systems. Such informal procedures are often the springboard for creating the opportunity to exercise autonomy, a key element in managerial life. In most management positions, even when there are external constraints, the manager has enough freedom from hour-to-hour supervision to be able to develop his or her own trusted relationships, informal defences against excessive routine, ways of investing tasks with meaningful personal influence, and so on.

From the point of view of strict time-and-motion studies or quantifiable computer-based systems design, some of these informal relationships and the desire for local autonomy may seem to be irrational, untidy and inefficient. They can, however, be highly productive because they help to motivate individuals and to keep the organization from falling apart. For example, as discussed by Michel Crozier in Chapter 5, central top management are rarely able to grasp the realities of local situations sufficiently well to be able to define precise operating criteria, immediate problems and information needs. The organization is able to adapt to different local needs because of the *creative intervention* of middle managers, supervisors and other staff in interpreting vague or ill-informed directives on the organization's behalf.

This informal diffusion of authority is an important motivational factor to middle managers and supervisors and is a valuable source of on-the-job training and experience. It also helps to reduce stress on senior management, who may not be emotionally or technically capable of shouldering the authority supposed by official job descriptions. It is also a key ingredient in promoting organizational flexibility, yet it is often unrecognized in formal descriptions of authority structures.

In tailoring new office technology to formal organizational concepts, it is often incorrectly assumed that the manager's job is a purely intellectual and rational exercise. Actually, managers operate amidst a mass of amorphous, conflicting and shifting perceptions and problems. These uncertainties do *not* arise just because information has been collected in a disorganized way, or is difficult to analyze and retrieve; an intrinsic aspect of management is that of handling the uncertainties about how people will behave.

Organizational inflexibility
Formal systems-design theories generally assume that management works with well-defined objectives and a clear evaluative scale, which can convert analytical information into a specific decision. In practice, as organization specialists Feldman and March have pointed out, much information is gathered 'in a surveillance rather than a decision mode'.[4] This means that information-gathering acts as a means of scanning the environment for signs of change, implying that organization strategies should be flexible to cope with new threats, challenges and opportunities. Goals are less fixed, more open to revision and less definite than assumed in formal notions of organizations and decision processes.

Managers therefore will wish to avoid being tied down to precise criteria by a computer-based system. Once incorporated into software, these aims and procedures become too rigid whereas informality, ambiguity and an element of secrecy can aid management effectiveness and organizational flexibility. As Michel Crozier has also pointed out in Chapter 5, managers need to develop skills of negotiation, persuasion and compromise to resolve the conflicting interests and perceptions which are an integral part of the decision-making process. The formal view of systems, however, tends to assume that there is a single decision-maker who analyzes, calculates and decides. It is taken for granted, incorrectly, that a decision equals the corresponding effect. Most decision-makers share influence, competence and authority with peers and subordinates. Between the decision itself and what is finally implemented, there can be varying degrees of constructive, creative intervention or even negative resistance. The process of enactment may be as arduous and complex as the original decision process, involving bargaining and trade-offs amongst many interest groups.

Deskilling and increased stress and alienation
Failure to give sufficient priority to the informal reality of managers' work can lead to a reduction in the use of vital management skills. The result will be a lessening of personal identification with the job, increased alienation and stress, and a consequent destruction of loyalty. This then creates a need for more external supervision and control, which exacerbates the anxiety and loss of motivation by some managers.

An influential management analyst, Harold Levinson, has summarized the most important management skills as follows:

> Managerial jobs involve a lot of contact with other people. Often this contact is unpleasant but has to be tolerated because of the inherent demands of the job. . . He or she must cope with the least capable employees, the depressed, the suspicious, the rivalrous, the self-centred and the generally unhappy. The manager must balance these conflicting personalities and create from them a motivated work group. He or she must define group purpose and organize people around that, resolve conflicts, establish priorities, make decisions about other people, accept and deflect their hostility, and deal with the frustration endemic to that continuing interaction. . . Many contemporary management situations provide the perfect breeding ground for cases of managerial burnout .[5]

A manager's most important effort is therefore poured into the intensely human processes of persuasion and bargaining. This is primarily an emotional challenge which is unlikely to be appreciably aided by information systems which formalize the intellectual aspect of decision-making. As Chris Argyris has observed, the introduction of new office technology requires more than technical competence. It needs, he says, 'knowledge about the human aspects of organization, such as personality, small groups, intergroups and living systems of organizational norms'. This emotional and interpersonal skill, he points out, has been undermined by the misplaced faith that rational information systems could be a 'technological fix' for the key management problems in increasingly complex organizational environments.

Computer-based systems whose software incorporates simplified and unrealistic assumptions can imprison managers in what Argyris has called 'psychological failure and double-bind'. Organizational success can mean personal failure for managers and vice versa because there is conflict between the manager's own perceptions and needs and those demanded by the system. When managers adapt to their new more formalized and mechanical roles, initiative and responsibility are lost; if they do not, they will be in constant conflict with the system. Either way, they will be under additional stress created by the dichotomy between the computerized expectations of human behaviour and the actual social and information interactions which shape the management process.

It is not only middle managers and supervisors who will face increased stress. If computer-based systems reduce the traditional emotional support and sharing of responsibility with subordinates, higher levels of management will be forced to exercise authority and responsibility on their own. While senior managers may be able to escape some external responsibilities by 'blaming the computer', their accountability within the organization could be sharpened even to an unrealistic (and for the manager on the receiving end, untenable) degree. This shifts the emphasis from power-based management to authority based on competence. In some ways it is a welcome change of emphasis, but could create immense pressure on managers who will have to survive in a world where competence, or the lack of it, is visible at all times.

Avoidance of risk taking
The increased formalization implicit in many computer-based systems could lead to a reduced willingness to take risks. People are more inclined to adopt high risk activities if they themselves control the outcome of the activity and the decision whether and when to enter it or withdraw from it. Formalization is often perceived as a means of reducing risk by imposing controls on other groups. In one court organization, for example, lawyers and social workers had to work with the same cases and information.[6] Each professional group had its own interests, perceptions and biases. The groups clashed over the information system design, each trying to impose formalization (and control) on the other, while retaining informality and flexibility for themselves.

My own investigations amongst managers have found that they believe that external manipulation and control are more likely if they are in an environment which places stress on computer-based systems programmed with formal, impersonal information flows and management processes. They feel far happier — and therefore more willing to take imaginative initiatives with some risk element — when engaging in informal activities with which they are familiar.

Emphasizing information quantity rather than quality

When faced with important decisions, managers often attempt to shed information and to simplify the problem to feasible dimensions[7]. This is not just an emotional response. The same pragmatic art of defining solvable, coherent problems underlies the thinking processes of scientists, who are exemplars of rationality.[8] Some justifications of the introduction of new office technology, however, assert that managers need *more* information to improve their effectiveness. Providing more information and analyses is not in itself a solution to management problems. In fact, it may add to a manager's sense of insecurity and incoherence because too much information may confuse and obscure the real difficulty, which is to understand the true nature of the problem. This can cause delay, increased stress and management ineffectiveness, particularly if the anonymous and impersonal computerized source makes it impossible to use personal contact and knowledge as a check on the credibility of the information.

Managers may often call for more information or decry the lack of it, while at the same time ignoring available data that would be relevant to the decision being taken. They may pay lip service to the general value given to formal information but, in practice, have their own informal notions of what is relevant. Additional analysis can be used to defend against failure or later criticism without ever being used beforehand to shape the decision.

Some information may also be collected for its symbolic value denoting competence and authority, for example to project an image of efficiency, security or safety (say, by an operator of a nuclear power station or a medicinal drug manufacturer). Such symbolic roles can support authority structures and group identities that maintain a sense of coherence. In some cases, the computerized system which provides this status is hardly used or may even be abandoned while still maintaining its symbolic significance (see the PERT example early in Chapter 6). The importance of information lies in its meaning and its relevance to real management and operational needs rather than in its quantity, which could be an irrelevant measure.

Increased organizational conflict

The introduction of new office technology offers opportunities and problems for different groups within the organization. Managers therefore need to handle an extra dimension of complexity in the organization which arises from having to accommodate to, and control, new interest groups created by the technology. Those members of the organization involved in designing a new information system enjoy positions of great influence, at least momentarily. The system itself can become a target for takeover by rival groups within the organization, often undertaken in a largely hidden, perhaps even unconscious, manner. The information system may therefore come to reflect and consolidate the views of the most influential groups, although the underlying principles and the interests which they serve are never made explicit.

When the implicit assumptions in the system design mesh with their immediate objectives, values and interest, users of the system will experience an euphoric sense of power, security and efficiency. They will, however, feel intense frustration, insecurity and loss of motivation if their perceptions are different from those built into the system. In situations where no single group has gained dominance over the information system, more overt conflicts could break out. Each group could acquire their own system or demand their own specialized use of the shared computing resource. For specific groups, this may mean more powerful and relevant services but their inward-looking and self-tuned nature could make communications between groups weaker and more incoherent than before, as well as creating problems of technical incompatibility.

An example of the incoherence that can develop occurred in an organization which installed an automatic text processing system, which was widely used throughout the organization. The software proved to be inadequate for the needs of different managers and also full of errors. Each manager autonomously created his or her own adaptation of the software to correct errors and to tailor it to local needs. The proliferation of many local programs was a positive factor in terms of allowing for local autonomy, but on the other hand, there was no longer a common basis for interdepartmental co-operative work. The overall system became literally incomprehensible to any one specialist who might be required to update it in the corporate interest. Managers also became so wrapped up in the mysteries of their own local system that their mobility within the organization became restricted and personnel recruitment became a more serious and costly task than before.

Conflicts can also develop between the specialists responsible for the technical development and the interests of managers and users. This can lead to the establishment of a new layer of bureaucratic committees to reconcile differences during the continuous correction, adaptation and updating of the system. Advice on how to handle such pluralistic demands within organizations is summarized by Rob Kling in Chapter 13. Niels Bjørn-Andersen in Chapter 7 also looks at possible conflicts that may arise in the changing relationship between managers and secretaries.

TURNING THREATS INTO OPPORTUNITIES

The radical technological and other changes in the environments in which organizations operate mean that organizations and the management roles which support them will need to adapt to new conditions. The potential for change should be recognized and openly analyzed to identify and implement its constructive and beneficial aspects. There are no intrinsic reasons why computer-based information systems should lead to the kinds of organizational and individual job degradation discussed so far in this chapter, such as loss of autonomy, deskilling, alienation and increased stress.

In order to use new technology to enlarge the scope and interest of managerial jobs, a strategy needs to be developed to counteract the threats to management effectiveness. A first step is to make explicit the assumptions used in systems design and development about the nature of the social entities involved — the organization, its constituent human beings, how they interact and what influences their behaviour. It should be recognized that technological change in offices involves essentially political processes rather than being a purely technical activity (see Chapter 2). Traditional management skills of negotiation, motivation and conflict resolution are needed to manage the change effectively, rather than professional competence in the technology.

The key to whether the system proves to be beneficial or harmful to management is the question of autonomy. Rob Kling has commented that managers who feel that new information systems have enhanced their work are those who have substantial discretion in their decisions about whether, when and how to use computing because they can utilize it as a relatively flexible resource to fit many social agendas.

The management of change should recognize that organizations consist of coalitions of interests and that the information systems should relate to local as well as central requirements. If this does not happen, either management will unwillingly obey a system which diminishes their traditional skills and motivations or else particular groups will create their own means of survival, alienated from the organization's overall values and purpose.

The design of the information system should recognize that such a diversity of interests and objectives, combined with the fundamental changes caused by the system itself, should lead to a *greater* emphasis on human negotiation and interpersonal skills. It should also explicitly recognize the importance of taking account of the emotional roots of many 'rational' actions, processes and responses.

Attention should be paid to developing skills in self-reflection and analysis of the informal and unofficial organizational structures and information flows. New insights will be gained into the organization, its authority structures and other aspects which will assist the systems design but are in any case useful knowledge. For example, upon reflection, it might become clear that periods of managers' slack time, on the surface detrimental to an individual's productivity, could actually be essential for the manager's emotional survival.

The technology itself is less of a problem than the overly simplistic assumption that 'technical fixes' can automatically avoid human considerations. A design process involving participation from all levels of management and staff, coupled with an evolutionary, sensitive and *selective* approach to their implementation, is likely to allow the proper and valuable uses of new office technology to be chosen rather than those situations where the role of the technology may be of questionable necessity or even be downright negative.

RECOMMENDATIONS

1 Recognize the importance of informal and unofficial organizational structures, processes and information flows to the maintenance of organizational flexibility and managerial motivation.

2 Identify the informal management patterns, their organizational roles and consequence, but do not use this analysis as a starting

point to formalize them. Their value to the organization and individual is *because* they are informal; the system should allow their continued existence.

3 Make a systematic attempt to develop management's ability to reflect on, study and express the emotional and human interactions which need to be taken into account when deciding on appropriate uses of new office technology.

4 Ensure that design, development, implementation and evaluation of new systems takes place with the active participation of all levels of management.

5 Encourage management to participate imaginatively and constructively by understanding and discussing their perceptions of the real social realities of the organizations and their own jobs.

6 Explicitly examine the key areas of computer-based systems that could adversely influence management effectiveness, for example in relation to factors such as autonomy; organizational flexibility; the tendency to concentrate power at the top and to cause corresponding middle-management alienation and deskilling; increased stress; less risk-taking; more central surveillance and control; too much concern with the quantity rather than quality of information; and extra complexity.

REFERENCES

1 Bird, E., 'Management Effectiveness: Aids to Communication in the Electronic Office' in Proceedings of *White Collar Productivity*, Communications Information Systems, the Yankee Group, Chorleywood, UK, 1980.

2 Pettigrew, A., 'Information Control as a Power Resource', *Sociology* No 6, pages 187-204, 1972.

3 Argyris, C., 'Double-loop Learning in Organizations', *Harvard Business Review*, No 55, pages 115-125, 1977.

4 Feldman, M., March, J.G., 'Information in Organizations as Signal and Symbol', paper to Annual General Meeting of the Western Political Science Association, San Francisco, 1980.

5 Levinson, H., 'When Executives Burn Out', *Harvard Business Review*, 59, pages 73-82, 1981.

6 Albrecht, G., 'The Effects of Computerized Information Systems on Juvenile Courts', *Justice Systems Journal*, No 2, pages 147-170, 1976.

7 Keen, P.G.W., 'Information Systems and Organizational Change', *Communications of the ACM*, 24, No 1, 24-33, 1981.# Minzberg, H., *How Managers Manage*, Harper and Row, New York, 1974.

8 Mulkay, M.J., *Science and the Sociology of Knowledge*, Allen and Unwin, London, 1980.

CHAPTER 9: NEGOTIATING TECHNOLOGICAL CHANGE

John Evans

INTRODUCTION

Experiences of introducing new office technology discussed earlier in the book have shown the variety of opportunities and problems which exist. Human and organizational goals can be reconciled with economic and technical objectives but the change process may produce different 'balance sheets' of gains and losses for different groups. Senior management, for example, will unconditionally welcome the technology's potential to improve efficiency, increase flexibility and extend the scope of centralized control. For other managers and staff, technology could provide varying degrees of mixed blessings (see Chapters 7 and 8).

In order to create a stable framework for technological innovation, different group interests, and economic and social goals need to be accommodated. This chapter examines the role of labour relations (industrial relations) systems in striving for an appropriate balance. It draws on experiences in Western Europe, the United States and Japan to identify the main types of laws, regulations and negotiating procedures adopted and the most common issues involved.

TRADE UNION ATTITUDES TO TECHNOLOGICAL CHANGE

In the periods of rapid industrial innovation in Europe in the nineteenth and early twentieth century, little account was taken of the social costs borne by those who were adversely affected by the change. Since then, trade unions have been established to represent working people, as a counter-balance to employers and managers.

The introduction of information technology has thrown into sharp relief the strong and weak points of national industrial relations systems. It is inextricably linked with other social, economic, organizational and political issues. The attitudes of unions to technology has therefore varied according to the state of these other factors, particularly the economic climate and the level of unemployment.

In the thirty years after the Second World War, faster change than during the Industrial Revolution took place in many countries. This was generally managed within a co-operative environment, by mutual agreement between unions and managers. It was a period of economic growth and relative prosperity. Although there were cases where new technology was resisted, for example in the printing industry, unions usually took the view that new technology should be introduced. Their main concern was to ensure that the whole workforce shared in the benefits of change. A report submitted to the 1966 Swedish Confederation of Trade Unions' Congress, for example, commented that 'The Swedish trade union movement has long taken a positive approach to technological change by suggesting a blueprint for structural policy designed to secure an increase in growth of the Swedish economy and formulating the basic security requirements for the individual in a changing society.'

In the early 1960s, concern was expressed in the United States that computer-based automation could increase unemployment. This worry diminished as the United States benefited from the industrial growth stimulated by the country's lead in computing and other technological industries. When the economic recession and a surge of unemployment hit the United States in the early 1980s, the debate about technology and unemployment re-emerged. This debate began in Europe in the mid-1970s, where the rise in unemployment happened sooner. By 1979, almost 50 per cent of the workforce in the Federal Republic of Germany (West Germany) were covered by agreements which gave special protection in cases of employment rationalization.

Unemployment is a weapon of fear. As unemployment mounted, unions began to adopt a more defensive attitude to technological innovation. Information technology was seen as a possible cause of long-term high unemployment because its impact occurs so quickly and over such a range of activities, particularly in offices which had been a major area of employment growth after the Second World War. Even in these difficult circumstances, however, many unions took a positive view of technology and the need to create new industrial policies to benefit from innovation. In 1975, for example, the metalworkers' union in West Germany, IG Metall, organized a conference about the watch industry, which was threatened by the switch to microelectronic from mechanical components. The conference triggered the introduction of government grants to assist manufacturers with restructuring, research and innovation to try to ensure long-term employment in this sector.

The strategic significance of information technology has meant that unions have regarded negotiations over its introduction as an opportunity to examine many issues which have long been the subject of bargaining with governments and management, such as the quality of the working environment, reductions in working time, career and training policies, public and private investment policies, public sector expansion and industrial democracy.

WAYS OF REGULATING CHANGE

The ways in which technological change has been regulated reflect the political, industrial relations and cultural environment of different countries. In Japan, for example, rapid industrial innovation has been stimulated because there is a strong consensus of view between government, larger private companies and their company-based unions, although problems have also emerged, as discussed later in the chapter. In the United States and Europe, the different strengths of white collar unions have been important in determining the nature of the response to information technology.

By the early 1980s, unions in the United States had failed to extend their membership significantly from their traditional base of skilled and semi-skilled blue collar workers into the rapidly expanding white collar and service sectors. Most agreements about new technology therefore were made in strongly unionized manufacturing companies, such as in the automotive industry. In Western Europe, however, white collar unions were much stronger. They have prepared a detailed 'agenda' of union requirements with various national approaches to turn the agenda into actions.

Jostein Fjalestad of the Norwegian Computer Centre has identified three main methods of joint management of change: *regulation* based on legislation, standards and rules; *negotiations* to conclude technology agreements; and *local developments* which encourage grassroots participation to ensure agreements are relevant to particular workplaces. Figure 9.1 summarizes procedures adopted in different countries. (Note that some of the laws may have been amended or superseded after the publication of this book.) Regulation, negotiation and local develop-

Country	Laws and Regulations	Collective Agreements		
		National Agreements	Sectoral level	Company or Plant Level
West Germany	Works Constitution Act 1972 Works Safety Act 1973 plus VDT regulations 1981	None	Job protection agreements in metalworking, textiles, footwear, leather, paper processing, printing	Over 100 agreements concluded
UK	Health and Safety at Work Act 1975	None	Parts of public sector	Over 200 agreements concluded
Norway	Working Environment Act 1977, plus VDT Regulations, 1982	1975 Employer/Union Agreement on computer-based systems	Banking	Most of industry and services covered by local agreements
Sweden	Working Environment Act 1978, plus VDT Regulations 1981 Codetermination Act 1977	1976 Employer/Union Work Environment Agreement	Technology agreement in printing. Codetermination agreements in public government & private industry.	Use of legislative rights
Various	Health and Safety laws (France, Italy and elsewhere) Codetermination laws (e.g. in Austria) Statute of Workers Rights 1970 (Italy)	1981 agreement for private sector in Denmark	Printing sector in Netherlands, Belgium, Austria and Greece; metal working in Italy	In USA, 1979 Ford agreement on procedures for introducing technology. General Motors quality of working life programme. In Japan, company unions consensus in return for job security and income sector.

Figure 9.1 Examples of procedures for joint regulation of technological change

ments should be regarded as complementary approaches. Laws and standards define minimum requirements. National, sectoral and corporate technology agreements establish the procedures and broad actions to be followed and the mechanisms to resolve conflicts. They set out the framework to be used in negotiating acceptable arrangements at local levels. Without genuine local agreement, however, the other methods will fail to achieve their aims.

Laws and national agreements are particularly useful in establishing standards on physical ergonomics (see Chapter 10). It is much harder for such generalized methods to come to grips with non-quantifiable but potentially more significant areas such as the software and psychological ergonomics discussed by Sigurd Jensen in Chapter 11. On these issues, knowledge resides with local work groups. Harnessing this local experience is a key factor in determining how new office systems are implemented. The encouragement of local participation in systems design and the shaping to the working environment has therefore been an important focus in negotiations.

An officer of the British white collar union ASTMS, Sheila McKechnie, has summarized the relationship between various negotiation procedures: 'Any trade union approach must be directed nationally to set the minimum standards and locally to educate staff representatives into enforcing these standards. Collective bargaining becomes the method whereby difficulties of implementation are resolved.'

The role of legislation

There are two key areas concerned with introducing new technology which have been affected by legislation — health and safety and 'codetermination'. Health and safety legislation usually takes the form of enabling Acts which lay down procedures and give official bodies the right to publish guidelines and standards, typically on the physical environment and equipment (such as VDTs) but also on broader aspects of working conditions. Codetermination legislation arises from moves towards 'industrial democracy'.

The 1977 Norwegian Work Environment Act, for example, empowers the Labour Inspectorate, an independent government agency, to issue binding regulations to ensure that 'the working environment is fully satisfactory as regards the safety, health and welfare of employees' and that 'technology and the work organization is designed so that employees are not exposed to undesirable physical and mental strain'.

The 1977 Swedish Act of Codetermination is an example of a comprehensive attempt to extend industrial democracy. It covers all major questions of management policy, including organizational and technological change. Employers are required by it to inform trade unions about plans for future developments and to initiate discussions and negotiations on new technology *before* any change takes place or any final decisions are taken on the nature of the system.

Legislation cannot, however, be regarded as a substitute for local agreements. In the United Kingdom, for example, the 1975 Employment Act proved ineffective in its intention to place an obligation on employers to disclose advanced information on major changes. A Trade Union Research Unit from Ruskin College, Oxford, discovered that, despite the Act, union representatives 'found it difficult to obtain information about proposed technological developments where there is no agreement to negotiate new technology at a local level'.

New technology agreements

Negotiations about the introduction of new technology are not new. They have been an essential ingredient in many agreements. In traditional manufacturing industries, however, the unions' main aim was to achieve satisfactory pay and conditions. They were not generally concerned with having a say in designing and applying the technology.

The first negotiations about computer technology occurred in the printing industry in the 1960s and 1970s. In some cases, such as at the *Washington Post* offices in the United States, computerized systems were introduced unilaterally by management. In many countries there have been prolonged and sometimes frequent strikes over new technology in printing. A strike in 1977-8 in West Germany, for example, eventually led to the signing of an agreement which contained various safeguards to assist printers in the transition to new technology, such as the provision of retraining and a guarantee of no downgrading of status for six years.

During the 1970s, a more coherent and comprehensive union approach towards negotiating about technology began to emerge. The union conception of these *new technology agreements* (or, simply, *technology agreements)* was to move away from the largely piecemeal, limited and reactive ways with which unions had previously responded to technological innovation. In many cases, unions were in the forefront of analyzing the likely impact of information technology throughout society and sought to use technology agreements as a means of taking an active role in determining how technology was applied. Technology agreements explicitly place on the agenda of collective bargaining a range of topics which affect all aspects of technological and organizational change.

The archetypal technology agreement, which influenced discussions and actions throughout the world, was the 1975 agreement between the national organizations in Norway representing management (NAF) and unions (LO). It states a principle which has been recommended frequently in this book: that the social effects of new technology should be regarded with equal importance to economic and technical considerations. Procedures were accepted for the way technology is to be introduced, including full provision of information, consultation with staff and consideration of the quality of the working environment.

This is an example of a *national framework* agreement. Other framework agreements have been reached covering particular sectors of industry or a group of companies. A chemical industry agreement concluded in 1979 in West Germany is an example of the types of issues involved in many sectoral agreements. It agreed to increased levels of redundancy pay, six months' earnings guarantee in the case of retraining, safeguards against sudden downgrading because of new technology and to lower the eligibility requirements for the industry's unemployment insurance scheme.

Some large public and private organizations have settled corporate framework agreements. For example, in 1979 the United Auto Workers and the Ford Motor Company in the United States established a national committee on the introduction of new technology. The company accepted that it would not use technology to undermine traditional bargaining units and local representatives were elected to monitor changes at plant level.

Local negotiations often tackle new technology by adding clauses to existing agreements; this is particularly true in areas like manufacturing production which has an established structure for coping with automation. The new breed of special technology agreements have, however, become increasingly used in company and plant negotiations, particularly in white collar jobs.

In the United Kingdom, for example, over 200 new technology agreements were identified in 1982 by the independent trade-union based research centre, the Labour Research Department (LRD).[1] The majority of these were signed after 1979, when the national union body, the TUC, issued guidelines to negotiators on technology agreements.[2] In its analysis of the actual agreements, the LRD found that most of them failed to meet some key TUC recommendations. For example, the TUC guidelines state that 'the case for accepting technological change rests largely on the fair distribution of the consequent benefits' but the LRD concluded that 'trade unionists have experienced few direct benefits either financially or in terms of reduced working time through the introduction of new technology'. On the other hand, the LRD found that, in white collar work at least, the aim of making technological change subject to discussion and agreement had been partly achieved, with only about one-third of responses saying that management had introduced new systems without consultation.

Unilateral action by management

There is another method of technological change to the ones outlined above: unilateral action by management. This can happen where unions are weak or where the threat of unemployment can be used to push through changes. It has frequently occurred in the United States with new office technology because of the low unionization of white collar staff. In fact it was pressure from union-stimulated ergonomics standards in Europe that has pushed American manufacturers to consider ergonomics as there was little pressure from American users. The unilateralist approach in the Unitd States has flourished because unionization of the workforce was only 20 per cent in 1980, compared to from 50 to 70 per cent in Western Europe.

Many employers view technology agreements an an interference with the 'manager's right to manage'. This sentiment was an important reason why the major employers' representative body in the United Kingdom, the CBI broke off talks with the TUC in 1980 to develop a joint statement on a 'framework for technological adaptation'. Unilateral action may sometimes succeed in getting new technology into an office or production plant in the short term. In the long run, however, management through force, fear, concealment or manipulation will be socially divisive as well as failing to achieve the optimization of social and economic goals. Most unions do not, as some managements fear, wish to use technology agreement negotiations to slow or block innovation. On the contrary, the general union aim is to use such agreements to provide an environment which will ensure long term employment security. This may mean that unions recognize the need to stimulate change and growth in industry and commerce and improved public services. Management could therefore view technology agreements as an opportunity rather than a threat.

Of course, if the overall economic and industrial relations climate is poor, unions may adopt negative and defensive postures. Managements who choose to take a unilateralist approach will exacerbate employees' suspicions, which could lead to conflict and various forms of resistance. As has been frequently stressed in this book (for example in Chapter 4), the success of new office technology depends on having co-operation and participation from all levels in an organization.

The Japanese approach

The success of Japan in managing economic growth with an apparently uncritical acceptance by the workforce of rapid technological innovation has led some people to look for a 'Japanese formula' which could facilitate change in other countries. There are many factors, however, which make the Japanese experience difficult to translate to other countries. On closer inspection, there are also some aspects of the Japanese system which seem undesirable. Japan has a dual labour market. About 35 to 40 per cent of the workforce are employed permanently in the 'formal' sector by large companies and public organizations. The rest work on short term contracts or on a daily casual basis in the private sector. About 20 per cent of the workforce of large companies are employed on such a basis to provide a flexible 'labour reserve'. The majority of people outside the formal part of the workforce are employed in smaller companies which supply goods to large firms. The large motor vehicle manufacturer, Toyota, for example, has several thousand subcontracting firms working for it. Production flexibility in larger companies is therefore often at the expense of subcontractors who change their stock levels, enter and leave business, hire and fire labour at a rapid rate and short notice.

The formal workforce belongs to company-based unions, which provide unswerving loyalty to the company. These employees have job security until the age of 55 and training and retraining is provided by the company with a strong emphasis on flexibility and a continuous acquisition of new skills in working life. Employee views of working procedures are solicited through 'quality circles', which discuss how to improve efficiency, and careers are governed by a seniority system, which ensures that status and pay are linked to length of service rather than a particular job or task. This provides a basis for great mobility and flexibility within a secure environment.

The rest of the workforce are generally not represented by unions, have lower wages and worse working conditions and no job security. These people are mainly women, older workers or those who failed to succeed in one of the schools which provide the entry route into formal sector jobs in large companies. Over 50 per cent of the female workforce is under 24 years old because there is a tradition in Japan that women work for only a few years before getting married. Older workers are often those who had received a lump sum pension on retirement from formal employment at the age of 55 but who are not yet receiving a State pension.

Some aspects of the arrangements in the formal sector are similar to union goals in technology agreements, such as job security, income guarantees when changing jobs, and staff consultation on the working environment. The dual nature of the Japanese system, however, would be unacceptable and undesirable in most Western industrialized countries.

There are also potential strains within Japan. If Japanese women become as determined as women in Western countries to have more equality at work, the current Japanese industrial relations systems would have to be altered radically. Increased unionization in the informal sector in Japan could break the consensus ideology in the formal sector. Spare capacity and unemployment hit some Japanese companies in the early 1980s, which began to make it more difficult to maintain even the limited 'lifetime employment' provisions in the formal sectors.

MAIN ELEMENTS IN TECHNOLOGY AGREEMENTS

Although technology agreements vary between and within countries, a number of ingredients are common to negotiations about new office technology. These can be divided into two categories: *procedural* and *substantive*. Procedural issues are concerned with the methods of introducing new technology and substantive issues relate to operational conditions once they have been implemented. The following is a summary of the main clauses that have been frequently discussed in technology agreement negotiations.

Procedural provisions in technology agreements
— A commitment by all parties to encourage the introduction of new technology and the successful management of change.

— The provision by management of full and timely information, in clear and jargon-free language, about plans for technological change. To be useful, the information must be provided at an early stage, before decisions are taken. It should be explicit about the likely effects of change and the options available.

— The establishment of joint management/union bodies to discuss, monitor and negotiate change at corporate and local levels.

— The opportunity for the election and training of 'technology representatives' or 'data stewards' with responsibility for monitoring the introduction of new technology on behalf of staff and who keep in close touch with grassroots experience and feelings.

— The arrangements by which unions can have access to outside expertise, just as management hires external consultants.

— The establishment of a procedure for monitoring and regulating the collection and use of personal data on individuals working in the organization.

— A *status quo* clause which gives the unions a right to veto changes unless they have been consulted and an agreement reached.

Substantive issues in technology agreements
— Job security following the introduction of new technology. This could aim to maintain the same number of job posts (total volume of employment) or, if some reduction in employment is unavoidable, to offer guarantees of no compulsory redundancy.

— The provision of adequate retraining opportunities to staff whose jobs are changed or eliminated by new technology and the establishment of guidelines on the maintenance of status and pay in the new job.

— Methods for sharing the benefits of new technology with employees through, for example, improved pay, shorter working hours and a better working environment.

— For older staff, the offer of adequate schemes for voluntary early retirement.

— Monitoring the impact of new technology on the workplace in terms of issues discussed in Chapters 7 and 11, such as stress, alienation, reduced social contact or increased central control and supervision.

— Health and safety regulations on aspects of working with computers, based on independent guidelines encompassing physical, software and psychological ergonomics factors.

— Protecting the confidentiality of personal information collected about employees and guaranteeing that such information will be limited to activities of direct relevance to work at the organization. Many countries have Data Protection legislation to provide the basic guidelines.

The impact on unemployment

Fears about *technological unemployment*, the replacement of people by computer-based systems, is at the emotional heart of employees' attitudes to new technology. Particular groups and individuals, who are threatened with being replaced by new technology, naturally take a defensive attitude. Technological unemployment explains why some jobs are lost. Technology on its own, however, does not explain how, when, and in what numbers jobs will be created. This depends on other economic, industrial, national and international policies and actions. The provision in technology agreements of at least some guarantees over job security, redeployment, training and voluntary redundancy helps to lessen these fears and to encourage change.

Negotiations at the workplace are primarily concerned with protecting existing jobs and providing safeguards for existing employees. In order to lessen general levels of unemployment and provide opportunities for newcomers to the workforce, a broader perspective is needed. Provisions in technology agreements for maintaining job levels, shortening working time and providing early voluntary retirement have been developed by unions to try to share out available work more equitably. The productivity improvements provided by information technologies are likely to mean that all countries will need to adjust to a period where even considerable economic growth could be accommodated while still leaving high levels of unemployment.

In practice, unions accept agreements which protect the existing workforce. For example, in a study of over a hundred technology agreements in the United Kingdom at the University of Aston, it was found that less than 10 per cent of agreements had a special commitment to maintain job levels. The most common protection was a 'no redundancy' clause, which means that no existing employee will be made redundant compulsorily. 'Attrition' and 'natural wastage', however, may mean that the total number of jobs are cut because people who leave voluntarily or retire may not be replaced.

In France one of the major trade union confederations, the CGT-FO, has argued that the computerization of society will be followed by a worsened employment situation if national and international industrial strategies are pursued independently of employment and labour relations policies. It recommended that governments should give priority to developing plans to cope with the potentially devastating effect of technology on employment in certain regions and sectors, to develop new areas of activity that meet social as well as industrial and economic goals, and to encourage studies to provide the basis of standards for protecting the quality of the working environment.

Information and consultation

Some countries have codetermination legislation which requires employers to provide information and to consult with unions and staff representatives on any technological changes. Under West German law, for example, any plant or company where there are more than five employees must have a *works council* composed solely of representatives of employees. The main collective bargaining mechanism in West Germany at national and regional level, however, takes place between employers' associations and union federations. Divorced from the mainstream of collective bargaining, works council representatives have found it difficult to use information disclosed to them to influence the introduction of new systems.

The provision of information is therefore not sufficient in itself. If consultation is to lead to staff having a real influence on the nature of technological change, information provision must be linked to effective local bargaining based on the strength of local units or by appeal to a central body for legal rights. The timing of the provision of information and its completeness have also been a contentious area in implementing general principles. Unions often feel that information has been provided too late and that in some large (particularly multinational) organizations it is difficult to get a comprehensive view of plans.

Participation in systems design

In 1977 in Italy, the manufacturer of office systems, Olivetti, and the National Federation of Metalworkers, FLM, reached an agreement which established the union's right to participation in negotiating work practices that result from technological change. The union wished to use these rights to decrease the monotony of certain jobs. The management's aim was to achieve a more flexible system of production to cope with the switch from mechanical to electronic components. The result was the creation of integrated assembly units which upgraded skills and job satisfaction for individuals while providing for the required flexibility of work structure needed by new electronic production methods. This illustrates how employees can participate in a positive way in the design of work organization associated with new technology.

When it comes to involvement in the kind of technical systems design process needed to develop and implement new office information systems, unions have recognized that participation is ineffectual unless there is adequate training and back-up support. In 1982, for example, an agreement was reached in Sweden covering 1.3 million workers, which aims to ensure that unions can provide effective support to local bargaining. A key provision is the right of unions to hire 'wage-earner consultants' to advise them on systems development; in some cases, employers have paid the fees of such consultants. The agreement also allows unions to undertake research on the impact of technology at the workplace. Unions have become involved in research projects, often in joint undertakings with universities, because they have realized the importance of gaining research evidence independent from employers.

Health and safety in the working environment

The most effective area of technology agreements relating to new office systems has been in establishing physical ergonomic standards, particularly for the construction and use of VDTs. Most agreements stipulate some aspect of VDT ergonomics, often backed by legislation and quasi-legal rules. Since the beginning of 1981, most agreements in West Germany, for example, have followed guidelines of the Industrial Injuries Institute. This is a joint union-employer body which has the right to issue regulations under the 1973 Work Safety Act. These regulations have been used as the basis for factory inspections and for settling insurance claims for health damage to an employee.

Even in the United States, where there is no codetermination legislation, management accepts staff involvement in influencing the work environment. General Motors, for example, has quality of working life programmes based on plant level groups, although they are isolated from the collective bargaining structure.

In addition to questions about the hardware ergonomics of VDTs, an important element in technology agreement is related to the time spent operating them. Surveys of over one hundred works council agreements in West Germany in 1978 and 1980 showed that most agreements had a maximum limit of four hours' work per day at a VDT. An agreement in Norway with the national telecommunications authority put a limit of two hours a day on working with a VDT. In the United Kingdom, the LRD survey mentioned earlier also found a maximum of four hours a day in many agreements, with rest periods for VDT operators varying from 10 minutes' break every hour to 30 minutes every two hours. The lack of consistency is because this type of qualitative factor has less clear-cut standards than for physical ergonomics.

RECOMMENDATIONS

Government actions
1 Provide an example of good practice in the government's own function as an employer.

2 Establish a macroeconomic environment with appropriate industrial and social policies that are conducive to accommodating technological change in a stable manner.

Management actions
1 Recognize the long-term benefit to the organization of participation and encourage representation of affected groups.

2 Provide early information on proposed changes, before decisions are made, in a form which is understandable and geared to user requirements. This will help to allay staff fears and to ensure that the system design takes real user needs into account.

3 Include an assessment of social and manpower effects into strategies for technological change and make these assessments available to staff representatives.

4 Negotiate and conclude appropriate technology agreements.

5 Evaluate the options available with respect to hardware, software and psychological ergonomic standards and guidelines with new office systems. Select the best possible combination.

Union and staff representative actions

1 Ensure the groups most affected by new technology have adequate representation and that there are representative bodies at plant, company, sector and national levels, as appropriate.

2 Co-operate with other unions and staff representative bodies affected by similar changes.

3 Devote sufficient resources to assist local representatives and work groups in using information on effects of changes and in making decisions on the options available.

4 Provide training courses on technological change and the implications for employment and the work environment.

5 Ensure that where staff technology representatives (data stewards) sit on joint technical and systems design committees, they have adequate research backup and, if required, access to independent external consultants.

6 Establish procedures to monitor change.

7 Provide for appeals to national level for the resolution of conflicts if local negotiations fail to reach agreement.

REFERENCES

1 *Survey of New Technology,* Bargaining Report 22, Labour Research Department, London, 1982.

2 *Employment and Technology,* Trades Union Congress, London, 1979.

BIBLIOGRAPHY

Recommended reading of relevance to the issues discussed in this chapter, in addition to the above references and to bibliographies for Chapters 4, 7, 10 and 11, include:

Fjalestad, J., *Information Technology and Participation: Problems and Experience*, Norwegian Computing Centre, Oslo, 1981.

Galjaard, J.H., *A Technology Based Nation: An Inquiry into Industrial Organising and Robotising in Japan*, Science publication No 3, Inter-university Institute of Managers, Delft, Holland, 1981.

Kato, Y., *Pattern of Labour Use in Japan*, Shenshu University, Shenshu, Japan, 1980.

Schaff, A., Friedrichs, G., *et al Microelectronics and Society — for Better or Worse*, Report to the Club of Rome, 1982. English version: Pergamon Press, Oxford.

ETUI Reports, *The Impact of Microelectronics on Employment in Western Europe in the 1980s*, 1979, and *Redesigning Jobs — Western European Experiences*, 1981, European Trade Union Institute, Brussels.

CHAPTER 10: ERGONOMIC REQUIREMENTS

Albert Armbruster

INTRODUCTION

New office technology is often introduced to 'improve productivity', but this objective is often nebulous (see Chapter 3) and ignores broad personal and organization objectives. A key element that should be considered is the 'ergonomic' design of office information systems and the physical working environment. These issues were brought into prominence by trade union concern with the possible health hazards of VDTs (see Chapter 9). Ergonomics has become increasingly accepted by management, staff representatives and technical designers as a crucial determinant of the effectiveness of office systems.

This chapter examines the physical properties of new office equipment and the office environment, which are the aspects of ergonomics most amenable to scientific measurement and analysis. It emphasizes practical guidelines for designing and implementing systems. Chapter 12 examines the psychological and software aspects of good ergonomic design.

WHAT IS ERGONOMICS?

Ergonomics aims to optimize the interactions between people and technology in the working environment. It brings together the systematic application of techniques from a variety of disciplines, such as physiology, engineering, psychology and sociology. Although 'ergonomic' techniques have been applied since people began working in an organized way, the interdisciplinary nature of the subject means that it has taken a long time to become established as a clearly demarcated science in its own right.

It was in the nineteenth century that ergonomics emerged as a systematic study. Initially, ergonomics was applied primarily as a means of raising work output with purely economic and mechanistic objectives. As a result, ergonomics became associated with 'scientific management' designs which focus on the most manifest and short-term economic improvements. It was only after the Second World War, with the development of methodologies such as socio-technical design, that 'humanization' became an important design criterion in its own right (see Chapter 4).

During the War, there was a tremendous amount of ergonomic research in military systems, such as in the design of aeroplane cockpits. This led to the creation of what is known in the United States as *human factors engineering*, although in Europe the term 'ergonomics' is used to encompass an expanding range of social and psychological aspects of workplace design.

Ergonomics for computer-based office systems

During the 1960s and 70s, ergonomists established a considerable body of research evidence concerning the physical aspects of equipment and the office environment. For a long time, there was a deplorable disparity between available knowledge and its degree of application in the world of work. This was true, even in areas such as the physical aspects of VDTs, where there are clear and unambiguous guidelines that could be followed. The transfer of ergonomic knowledge from research to the field has been hampered by the short-term objectives and vaguely defined scope which characterized early ergonomics work. In addition, few educational and training courses had been supplied to management, professionals, staff and technical experts involved in designing and implementing computer-based systems. Some manufacturers did attempt to implement ergonomic principles but they tended to test the equipment in laboratory environments rather than in actual offices, so the final products were inadequate.

Ergonomics in computing systems began being paid more attention in the mid-1970s, largely because of efforts in Europe, particularly in Scandinavia and the Federal Republic of Germany, to introduce national standards and agreements as part of the process of negotiating technological change (see Chapter 9). When microelectronics caused computing systems to become available at the fingertips of a vast number of people, manufacturers and systems designers realized that appropriate ergonomic design and study was needed to ensure that this complex technology could be understood and used quickly and effectively by people with little or no prior training.

Costs associated with ergonomics

The need to cater for ergonomic criteria sometimes appear to add to the investment in new technology. I have known cases where changes to the office environment have been equivalent to the costs of the hardware and software. Many of the environmental changes, however, should have been provided in the office before new technology was introduced, such as adequate desks, chairs, lighting, climate and noise controls.

Some manufacturers have regarded ergonomics as a costly, optional extra. Equipment does indeed cost more if ergonomic needs are grafted onto it at a late stage in its development. If human factors criteria are built into the design of the equipment from its inception, however, there should be little, if any, cost differential. When considering apparent ergonomic 'overheads', users should evaluate the costs of *not* having appropriate systems and office environments — staff unhappiness, poor operation efficiency, resistance to the technology and increased absenteeism through physical and psychological stresses and strains.

In some environments, such as in universities and software development groups, ergonomic considerations have been virtually ignored without complaints from staff and without seeming to incur any penalties in work performance and staff motivation. Such people, however, are highly motivated to use computers and may be suffering from undetected longer-term health effects, such as eye strain and backache. Other staff working in offices are unlikely to accept such conditions.

As the cost of computing comes down, the total cost of an 'advanced' office with new technology is likely to be only about 10 to 20% more than a traditional, non-mechanized office, including all hardware and software. Ergonomics causes 'unnecessary' extra expenses only when the user or manufacturer fails to take adequate account of human factors principles at the inception of an office system project or the design of a new piece of equipment.

ERGONOMIC STANDARDS FOR OFFICES

Many countries have developed various standards relating to office workplaces. The majority of such standards have tended to concentrate on purely safety and technical aspects, such as electrical hazards and the dimensions and material properties of equipment. With computer-based systems, the main focus has been on VDTs.

Standards tend to be either general and qualitative or very detailed and quantitative. A Norwegian regulation, for example, specifies simply that, 'Screens should be adjustable for luminance (brightness) and contrast'. Such a qualitative approach can be contrasted tó a safety regulation in the Federal Republic of Germany, which states: 'In negative presentation (light symbols on a dark background) the contrast must lie between 3:1 and 15:1, better between 6:1 and 10:1. . .' A compromise solution could be to have overall qualitative guidelines backed by detailed measurements.

Despite the proliferation of national standards and recommendations, there are few standards at international levels. The supranational Comité Europeén de Normalisation (CEN), for example, took many years to produce an agreement on something as relatively simple as office desks. The main impact of standardization is therefore likely to come through national efforts or specific multinational programmes, such as INSIS (see Foreword).

WORKPLACE DESIGN

Some ergonomic aspects are similar for offices with or without computer-based technology, such as the requirements for noise level, room climate, chairs and desks. Higher demands are made on the lighting needed to prevent annoying reflections on a VDT screen. As some office technology equipment generates a significant level of heat and static, additional environmental control systems may be needed, although newer electronic systems have less additional impact on the environment than older equipment.

Figure 10.1 illustrates the key features of a VDT workplace. An important aspect is the adjustability of furniture and equipment to the user's own particular characteristics. The posture of the user is particularly important. Any posture which has to be maintained over a long period creates a 'static' load which is much more tiring than the load induced by movement. This has led to the notion of 'dynamic sitting', which allows for shifts in posture so that the load is spread to different parts of the skeletal (arms, spine, pelvis, legs) and muscular (neck, back, abdomen, arms, legs) systems. Faulty postures lead to distress and fatigue, which cause poor work performance, and to irreversible and often serious physiological ill-health.

An excess of adjustability can, however, be confusing to the user. Adjusting workplace components (like chairs and desks) is often employed in the first few weeks of use and can then be left in wrong positions. They should therefore be checked regularly by trained personnel.

Siting equipment on the desk top

Equipment and other items involved in work activities must be located to take into account the convenience and comfort of the user and the importance and frequency of the task. For example, the screen is generally placed directly behind the keyboard with the document holder to one side. In some activities where the operator is keying-in information, the document is the prime source of information with the screen used only to verify input; the document holder in such circumstances would be better placed directly behind the keyboard.

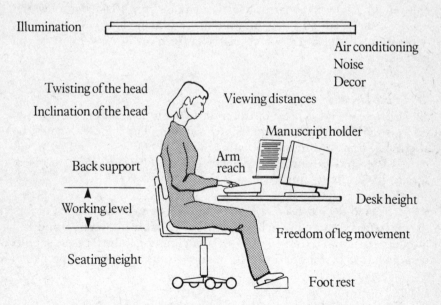

Figure 10.1 Important aspects in designing office workplaces

The following aspects should also be considered in the siting of work items:

— viewing distances to different items should be minimized (within an angle of 15 to 30 degrees relative to normal viewing) to prevent excessive eye, head and trunk movements;

— All equipment and items which must be manually manipulated should be within the normal arm reach of the operator;

— The operator should generally be working in a posture with the head inclined at an angle of about 20 degrees, the spine slightly arched forwards, upper arms vertical and forearms approximately horizontal, thighs horizontal and lower leg approximately vertical.

Working level

The working level (see Figure 10.1) is the distance between the underside of the thighs and the palms of the hand on the middle alphabetical row of keys. It should be between 220 and 250 mm. The recommended thigh clearance is 190 mm, which leaves 30 mm each for the desk top and keyboard height, which are available with modern equipment. Older keyboards, however, can be from 40 to 90 mm, which means either reducing leg movement or placing the keyboard in a depression in the desk, which restricts freedom of movement of the keyboard.

Desks and footrests

The European (CEN) standard for desk height is 720 mm. Adjustable tables should be in the range 680 to 760 mm. The leg area should be about 690 mm (minimum 650 mm) high and 800 mm (minimum 580 mm) wide, and free from any obstructions. The surface of the desk should have a matt finish.

When a fixed desk is used, a footrest should be provided which covers the entire leg area and which should be adjustable between 40 and 110 mm in height and 5 and 15 degrees in inclination. The footrest should be adjustable by foot action with a surface that prevents slipping.

Chairs

All office chairs should have the following features:
— good stability, typically provided by a five-point base with self-locking castors;

—easily adjustable seat height;

—easily adjustable backrest—for height and moving backwards and forwards;

—rounded seat front edge and padded seat surface with a covering in a textured material.

There are other options which may be desirable in certain circumstances, such as armrests, adjustable seat angle and backrest angles. There is a danger, however, that the provision of too many variations will lead to faulty adjustments. Care should be taken in the use of special 'gadgets', such as ribbed backrests which are supposed to initiate reflexes in the spine. These may be satisfactory for most users but may harm people with orthopaedic problems.

Document holders and documents

The document holder is often regarded as an 'insignificant' item of equipment, yet it could play an important role in reducing postural strain. The lack of attention paid to their construction, siting and the nature of the documents used with them, frequently cause the document holders to be rejected or discarded after a short time. The following considerations should therefore be borne in mind:

—holders must be unaffected by vibration;

—motor-driven paper feed is preferable because the reading area remains at a fixed height, as with a typewriter;

—if a fixed document position is provided, a transparent ruler, capable of being moved by a foot pedal, should be provided as a reading aid and the angle of the holder should not be too steep;

—the tablet backing the holder must be opaque;

—paper surfaces must be matt and with plain backgrounds.

VDT SCREENS

Characters are typically generated on a screen by using a Cathode Ray Tube as an electronic 'gun' focused onto a phosphor-coated inner lining on the screen. When the beam hits a phosphor point, it lights up; these points can be grouped to form characters. As soon as the image is formed, however, it begins to fade, so it has to be constantly refreshed. The speed at which this is done is called the *refresh rate*.

As the screen size often cannot accommodate the full text of a document, the display can be regarded as a 'window' on the document which can be *scrolled* — moved vertically (up and down) or horizontally (left and right) to scan areas outside the immediate 'frame' shown on the screen. Some systems can display *multiple windows* or *split screens* so that all or parts of more than one document can be shown on the screen.

Screen design and brightness control

— The screen should be detached from the keyboard and capable of being adjusted vertically and horizontally. If the screen is fixed to the keyboard, it should be approximately vertical to minimize reflections from it.

— The screen size (number and width of lines capable of being displayed) should be sufficient for the task. The height-to-width ratio *(aspect ratio)* should be 3:4 for horizontally mounted screens and 4:3 for vertical screens. Vertical *full page* screens can display the contents of an A4-size page.

— Viewing distance should be 300 to 800 mm.

— The image on the screen should be stable. This means having a refresh rate of at least 50 Hertz (Hz) in Europe and 60 Hz in the United States to avoid 'flicker'. If the screen has black characters on a white background (known as *positive* presentation), a rate of at least 80 Hz is needed. (A Hz is a unit of frequency equal to one cycle per second.) Poorly adjusted components and circuitry can cause the image to 'dance' from place to place on the screen; the equipment should therefore be serviced regularly by skilled personnel.

— The brightness or *luminance* (the amount of light reaching the eye from the screen) should be adjustable. The minimum luminance is 45 candela per square metre (cd/m^2) adjustable preferably between 80 and 160 cd/m^2; *candela* is a measurement of light intensity. Character images should remain sharply defined at maximum luminance.

— The characters should be lighter than the screen background (unless the refresh rate is sufficient to allow positive presentation), with a luminance contrast between 3:1 and 15:1, preferably 6:1 to 10:1. The contrast between the screen background and other items in the working field of view, such as documents, should be between 1:3 and 1:5 but 1:10 is acceptable. White, yellow and green characters are preferred, on appropriate backgrounds, or positive presentation.

— Reflections and glare from the screen should be avoided by having an anti-reflex coating on the screen and ensuring that the VDT is used with adequate lighting and curtaining. If character legibility is to be tested without special meters, the VDT should be placed near a window, which is its most difficult siting from a lighting point of view.

— Appropriate horizontal and vertical scrolling should be provided, preferably via *smooth* scrolling so that the text does not move jerkily on the screen.

— Split screens and multiple windows should be available if appropriate to the task being performed.

Character formation
— Text should be displayed in upper case (capitals) and lower case.

—Characters and symbols must have good *legibility* (the ability to detect and discriminate between individual characters) and *readability* (the ability to interpret and understand information). Legibility depends on a combination of character height and viewing distance, as shown in Figure 10.2. Increasing character size does not necessarily improve legibility, because larger characters can appear blurred on a screen.

— The *dimensions of characters* should be 3 to 5 mm in height with the minimum width 50% (preferably about 70%) of the height. The stroke width in characters like 'e' and 'a' should be 10 to 17% of the height of capital letters. The space between characters should be 20 to 50% and between rows 100 to 150% of the character height.

—For legibility and readability it must be possible to distinguish between the following characters:

X and K	S and 5	I and L	I (letter) and 1 (digit)
T and Y	U and V	O and Q	O (letter) and 0 (digit)
2 and Z	B and R	C and G	B (letter) and 8 (digit)

—The descenders on lower case characters (such as 'y' and 'p') should project below the base line for the bottom of capital letters.

—When a character is generated as a matrix of dots, it should have resolutions of 7 x 9 dots or more, rather than 5 x 7 dots. The dots should merge well to produce a well defined image.

—The character set should be sufficiently broad to encompass all the important characters and symbols used in a task.

—Basic characters should be upright but cursive *(italic)* sets are useful for some tasks.

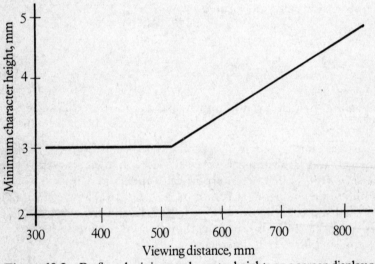

Figure 10.2   Preferred minimum character heights on a screen display as a function of viewing distance

Character coding
Information on the screen can be coded to highlight particular areas, words or items *(fields)* within a fixed format. This can be done by

differently coloured characters, varying brightness levels, flashing or blinking of words or *reverse video* (turning dark characters on a light background into light characters on a dark background and vice versa. Care should be taken to avoid causing confusion in the user by having too many variations on the screen at once. The following characteristics should be considered.

—The *cursor*, which is a pointer to the place in the text where the next character keyed-in will be placed, should be clearly distinguishable from other characters. It should be possible to suppress the repeated blinking action of the cursor.

—Under good lighting conditions, up to ten different colours could be tolerated on a screen but it would be preferable to have no more than six. Four colours would be a maximum in poor lighting.

—No more than three brightness levels should be attempted as a form of coding, although only two is preferable. Different brightness levels must be distinguishable at maximum luminance.

—Blinking should be at between 2 and 4 Hz.

—Different sizes and styles of characters should be capable of being displayed on the same screen.

—Information should be presented in the optimum screen area and should not, for example, be in the lower edge of the screen.

—The screen format should be consistent with other documents. For example, certain fields could be 'protected' to be the equivalent of a preprinted heading on an order form. Information on the screen should be in the same layout as on a printed form.

VDT KEYBOARDS

Keyboarding is a complex process in which movement of the hands and fingers are controlled by the brain in response to a variety of signals. Three basic types of feedback can occur during keying to inform the operator that the intended action has been taken and to aid in detecting errors: *tactile* responses based on the sensations of touch, position and movement; *auditory* signals and *visual* stimuli.

The speed of keying depends on many factors, such as keyboard layout, print/display mechanism and the training of the operator. The traditional QWERTY keyboard layout was designed for traditional manual typewriters with a basket print mechanism and was optimized to avoid keys becoming stuck. Other layouts by designers such as Levasseur, Meier and, probably the best, Dvorak, are more efficient. There have also been national adaptations of QWERTY, such as QWERTZ in Germany, which are widely used in Europe. The amount of training and experience invested in QWERTY means that this layout is still the most popular.

Typing speeds on manual and electric typewriters was increased by replacing the basket of keys with single element print devices, such as the *golfball* or *petal (daisy wheel)* mechanism. The golfball has the print characters arranged around a sphere; the daisy wheel has characters at the ends of petal-like spokes which spread from the hub of the wheel. The required character is positioned by rotating the sphere or wheel. Single element devices can be changed to provide a variety of type faces.

Typing errors decrease the speeds and increase the amount of keying. There are five main types of error: substituting a wrong character for a correct one; omitting text during keying; transposing characters in the wrong order; inserting superfluous keystrokes; and (particularly with word processors) command errors causing incorrect initiation of a system procedure. A large proportion of errors occur in the current line being printed. That is why even electronic typewriters with a single-line screen display can result in significant improvements in typing throughput. Screen-based word processors provide an even greater opportunity for improving typing throughput.

Whatever the design of the keyboard and display mechanism, pauses are always likely to cater for an operator's needs. When typing, people employ short-term memory in the brain to keep information of immediate need. If the text being typed contains chunks of difficult to remember information, like many digits, the short-term memory is capable of holding only a little data, so more time is spent reading and checking material.

Longer intervals will also occur if the operator is keying original material being generated during typing than when transcribing information, as a copy typist would do. The question of response time with computer-based systems is discussed in more detail in Chapter 11.

Construction of keyboard
—A VDT keyboard should be detached from the screen.

—The angle of the keyboard should be no more than 15 degrees to avoid an excessive load on the hand and arm. The height of the middle row of alphabetic keys should be less than 30 mm, which means a maximum distance from this row of keys to the underside of the desk top of 60 mm, see Figure 10.3. For keyboards higher than 30 mm, an adjustable handrest 50 to 100 mm deep and as wide as the keyboard should be provided.

—The width of the keyboard should not be greater than the size determined by the optimum key layout. Unnecessarily wide keyboards could mean that paper placed next to it causes fatiguing torsion of the head-neck-torso system.

—The surface of the keyboard should be matt finished. The reflectance of the keyboard and keys should be from 15 to 75% although 20 to 50% is preferable. The luminance ratio between keyboard, screen and documents should be less than 3:1 and not greater than 10:1.

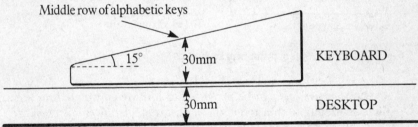

Figure 10.3 Preferable dimensions for keyboard and desk top

Keyboard layout
—The layout of the alphabetic keys should be the same as for the conventional typewriter (typically QWERTY) unless there is a clearly defined requirement, accompanied by appropriate training, to use a special layout.

—Where numeric keying plays a minor role, the digits should be laid out in a single row above the alpha keys, in the same way as conventional typewriters. If there is a great deal of numeric information input, a special block of numeric keys should be provided in addition to, or instead of, the numeric line above the alpha keys. Such a block should be as in Figure 10.4. Both these layouts are preferable to a single row. The telephone layout is particularly efficient with low-skilled operators when key-pad telephones are also used as part of the system. If numeric keying plays a dominant role in input, a detached numeric pad should be provided so that it can be sited conveniently for left and right-handed users.

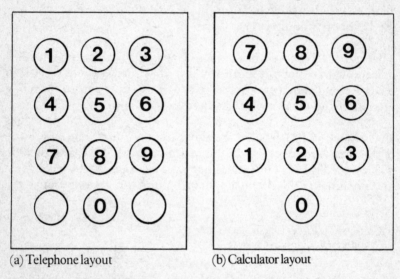

(a) Telephone layout   (b) Calculator layout

Figure 10.4   Layouts of numerical keyboards

—Special *function keys* can be provided to initiate complete functions, such as 'delete a character' or 'send an electronic mail message'. Too few or too many function keys could impede users, so the number and type of such keys should be optimized to the task. Their arrangement should correspond to the sequences followed in the task.

—Keys which relate to different functions should be made distinct through their colour and/or shape and/or position. The most important function keys should be colour coded.

—Cursor control keys should be in a group relative to the direction of movement initiated. The key which moves the cursor to the left should be on the left of the group; the upwards movement should be by a key at the top of the group; and so on.

Characteristics of keys

—The shape of the key should aid accurate location by the finger tip, minimize reflections and provide a suitable surface for key *legends* the labels describing the keys' functions. They should prevent the accumulation of dirt and moisture and be comfortable to press. The surface of the key should therefore have a matt finish and be profiled in the manner illustrated in Figure 10.5 The profiles in (a) and (b) in this figure minimize reflection.

—The space between key centres should be between 18 and 20 mm. Each square key should be 12 to 15 mm square; the top of *mesa* keys (Figure 10.5a) should be about 9 mm square.

—No more than two legends should be on the key surface. They should be moulded into the keytop, rather than printed on it to ensure they are resistant to wear and abrasion. As the keyboard should be about the same distance from the eye as a VDT screen, the recommended character height for legends is also about 3 mm. Where appropriate, the label should be the same as for equivalent functions on typewriters. Function keys should avoid unintelligible abbreviations and codes except where standard symbols are easy to understand, such as the arrows to indicate the direction on cursor control keys.

—Black or white should be avoided as background key colours because they give bright reflections. In general, legends should be darker than the key top. For frequently used alphanumeric keys, the background should be in a neutral colour, such as beige, ivory or

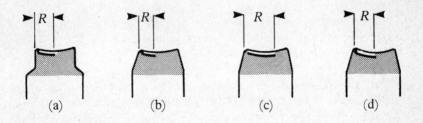

R - Reflective part of the keytop

Figure 10.5   Keytop profiles showing reflection areas with inadequate lighting

light grey. Legibility on function keys which require discrimination
from other keys can be provided with pastel coloured key surfaces.
Single keys or small groups of keys which need special highlighting
could be in bright colours, even if they exceed reflectance restrictions.

—The keytops should be cleaned regularly.

The keys in operation
  —The force required to depress a key should be 0.25 to 1.5 newtons
   (N); a newton is a unit of force. The key should need to travel by
   from 0.8 to 4.8 mm to be activated.

—Auditory and tactile feedback should be provided. A short 'click'
  sound is sufficient. More penetrating and longer sounds can be
  intolerable when used for normal feedback but are rightly used to
  inform operators of important errors and other activities that need
  urgent attention. A short snap-action mechanism provides
  sufficient positive tactile feedback to let the user know that the
  intended operation has been carried out. Such feedback is
  particularly important for less skilled operators or infrequent users.

—Various safeguards should be provided against faulty or accidental
  keying. Where incorrect action of a key could have serious consequences, precautions could be taken, such as requiring a stronger
  force than usual to activate the key; demanding that the key should
  be depressed more than once; using a special key-lock; positioning
  the key in a special place; or requiring that the function be initiated
  by two or more keys. To avoid errors caused when skilled users
  input a burst of overlapping keystrokes, an *n-key roll-over* capability
  should be provided which stores all keystrokes and then generates
  them in the correct sequence.

—*Self-programming 'soft' function keys* should be provided to help
  tailor the system to special needs. They perform the function
  specified by the user.

—*Repeat* and *typamatic* keys enable certain characters to be input
  continuously. A repeat key needs to be depressed at the same time as
  the key to be repeated. Typamatic keys repeat automatically after
  being depressed for a given period, typically over half a second, and
  are useful for a few characters, like underlining and the letter 'X'.

— Particular care should be taken in the functioning of the 'delete' or 'kill' key. An 'undelete' or 'wastebin' facility should be provided to enable information to be retrieved for a set period after deletion.

VDT SYSTEMS REQUIREMENTS

— If there is a system or VDT malfunction, a clear audible or visual signal must be given to the operator.

— The state of the VDT should be clearly indicated to the operator by a continuous light, for example, showing whether the terminal is sending or receiving information. Flashing light indicators are advisable to draw attention only to critical events.

— The response time should be less than two seconds and the operator should be warned if there is a long or variable delay (see Chapter 11).

— Regular care and maintenance should be provided to all aspects of the VDT, including the screen and keyboard.

PRINTING DEVICES

There are two main techniques for creating printed *hardcopy* output — *impact* and *non-impact*. Impact printers create images by making a physical impression on paper, such as with a manual typewriter basket or a golfball or daisy wheel element. Non-impact printers create images on paper in different ways. For example, *ink jet* printers squirt ink droplets at high speed. *Electrosensitive* and *thermal* printers require special paper to create impression using principles of static electricity and heat. *Laser* printers create character patterns using laser beams. Impact printers tend to be lower speed (typically about 30 to 40 characters a second) but of higher quality.

Two important ergonomic factors of printers are noise and legibility of output. Daisy wheel printers have a noise level of 60 decibels (dB(A)), which is satisfactory but other low speed impact printers have noise levels of between 70 and 90 dB(A), which are unsuitable for normal office environments unless noise-absorbing castings and/or foundations are used. Non-impact printers have a much better noise level and some systems are virtually silent. *Matrix* printers, which create characters as groups of dots made by needles, can have reasonable noise levels but have a high frequency acoustic emission which can be annoying or even detrimental to health.

OTHER OFFICE EQUIPMENT

Many of the principles described above for VDTs could apply to other equipment. Guidelines on clarity and legibility of screen displays, for example, are also applicable to microfilm and paper. It should be remembered that microfilm and VDTs create their images by emitting light whereas print and handwriting on paper are made visible by the different reflection properties of the ink and paper. The contrasts of character and background with paper therefore vary far less than with light-emitting displays, where an increase of incident lighting leads to loss of contrast.

New forms of input and output devices are being produced rapidly, such as computerized voice understanding and synthesized speech. Ergonomic standards will be developed after there has been sufficient time to study their application. In the meantime, ergonomics objectives should be applied to all new equipment, even if initially they are primarily subjective and qualitative, for example, requiring that synthetic voice equipment pronounce words distinctly and unambiguously and resemble human rather than machine sounds.

General criteria such as noise level, minimum heat emission and ease of use can apply to all other items of equipment, such as photocopiers or dictation equipment. If general noise levels are too high, typists using dictation equipment may turn up the volume so loud as to damage their hearing.

GENERAL ENVIRONMENT

The equipment must satisfy all international and local national safety standards. Electrical equipment must be safeguarded against the discharge of static electricity. Sufficient maintenance access must be provided to the workplace and all supply cables and other services to computers and VDTs should be concealed.

Lighting
In an office with artificial lighting, 300 to 700 *lux* (lx) is recommended for VDTs, with an optimum of 500 lx, although variations from 100 to 1000 have been suggested for other equipment (a *lux* is a unit of measure of illumination of a surface). An illumination as high as 1000 lx would be acceptable only if there are no VDTs, microfilm or other light-emitting devices.

To avoid direct glare, the light source should have neutral-white fluorescent lamps and should be shielded with grid or louvre patterns; prismatic or smoked glass shielding may also be suitable. The VDT workplace should be parallel to light sources and windows.

Curtains (with a reflectance from 50 to 70%), external or internal window blinds and louvres help to reduce glare and control the room climate. The average ceiling reflectance should not exceed 70%; the walls should be between 50 and 70% and the floor about 20%. The operators's field of vision should be free of direct reflections.

Room climate
—Exhaust air from equipment should not be trapped under the desk, in corners or directed towards neighbouring workplaces.

—Room temperature should be between 21 and 23 degrees C (maximum 26 degrees) and relative humidity should be from 50 to 65%.

—The speed of air movement at neck, waist and ankle should be less than 0.15 metres per second.

Noise
Noise levels should be less than 55 dB(A) in areas requiring a high level of concentration and less than 70 dB(A) in routine task areas. Equipment noise should be no more than 5 dB(A) above background noise, except for higher pitched audio signals and feedback from the VDT and other equipment.

HEALTH ASPECTS OF VDTS

Health deficiencies associated with VDTs are typical of most office workplaces. There is little scientifically corroborated evidence to show that the main new component of the VDT, the Cathode Ray Tube, is solely responsible for health problems. This should not, however, lead to a complacent attitude. The guidelines specified earlier in this chapter are needed for health reasons as well as for efficiency and job satisfaction.

Up to about 50% of the working population have uncorrected or inadequately corrected eyesight, although VDT operators naturally put down any eye strain to the equipment. If there is too much glare from the screen or other bad ergonomic features, the VDT could exacerbate eye problems. VDT operators should therefore be given regular eye tests.

An examination should be given before work begins on the VDT. This should consider the nature and duration of work and type of spectacles used as well as a thorough eye test. Spectacles for VDT work should be corrected for a viewing distance of 450 to 600 mm, preferably for 500 mm. For operators under 45, eye tests should be repeated every 60 months; for people over 45 years, every 36 months. If complaints occur in the meantime, intermediate tests should be carried out.

Special eye characteristics to be looked at are the ability to focus sharply in the near range; the absence of heterophoria (discrepancy between focusing and convergence distances) and 'colour blindness' with colour VDTs (about 1% of females and 8% of males suffer from this problem.

RECOMMENDATIONS

1   Support should be given by users, manufacturers and national and international bodies to the development of soundly-based ergonomic standards and to their implementation and continuous monitoring.

2   Management should insist on good ergonomic guidelines in the selection of equipment.

3   Unions and staff should become well versed in the principles and agreed standards of ergonomics to reduce or prevent difficulties during implementation and operation.

4 Management, unions and others involved in negotiating technological change should rely on well-researched standards as the basis for agreements.

5 Manufacturers should produce ergonomically optimal systems. They should make available in their literature ergonomic data specified in this chapter, in internationally accepted units of measurement.

6 The above recommendations could be achieved within the context set by established standards, recommendations and legal or quasi-legal regulations which provide maximum flexibility for users without unduly hampering the manufacturer.

7 Revision of such ergonomic guidelines should take place at regular intervals to incorporate new scientific evidence.

BIBLIOGRAPHY

The following books are of relevance to topics discussed in this chapter.

Cakir, A., Hart, D., Stewart, T.F.M., *Visual Display Terminals,* John Wiley & Sons, London, 1980. (German version) *Bildschirmarbeitsplätze,* Springer Verlag, Berlin-Heidelberg-New York, 1980. (French version) *Les Terminaux a Écran,* Les Editions D'Organisation, Paris, 1980. (Italian version) *Il Terminale Video,* Associazione Culturale Progresso Grafico, Turin, 1981.

Gradjean, E., Vigliani, E., (eds), *Ergonomic Aspects of Visual Display Terminals.* Taylor and Francis, London, 1980.

Johannsonn, G., Aronsson, G., *Stress Reactions in Computerized Administrative Work,* Reports from the Department of Psychology, University of Stockholm, 1980.

Smith, M.J., and others, *An Investigation of Health Complaints and Job Stress in Video Display Operations,* National Institute for Occupational Safety and Health (NIOSH), Cincinatti, Ohio, 1981.

Stewart, T.F.M., *Eye Tests for VDU operators,* V.E.T. Advisory Group, Loughborough University of Technology, UK, 1979.

CHAPTER 11: SOFTWARE AND USER SATISFACTION

Sigurd Jensen

INTRODUCTION

Physical ergonomics, as discussed in the previous chapter by Albert Armbruster, is concerned mainly with so-called 'objective', quantifiable ergonomic factors. There are other aspects of human factors design, such as psychological and software ergonomics, which relate more to the subjective perceptions and reactions of users (see Chapter 7).

This chapter looks further at the social and psychological dimensions of ergonomics. It explains why many of the problems caused by new technology in the office are created at the planning and design stages. Some of the physical and mental stresses experienced by operators of VDTs are discussed. Principles for the design of software dialogues between the user and system are examined.

PSYCHO-SOCIAL IMPACT OF NEW OFFICE TECHNOLOGY

Inadequate systems and software design can cause many staff problems such as physical strain and psychological stress. A decisive stage in planning computer systems is the specification of the criteria which will be used to guide and evaluate systems development. Figure 11.1 indicates some typical 'psychological job demands' that should be considered in the early phases of planning[1]. This is not an exclusive list and other factors could be specified. Whatever criteria are included, such psychological requirements should be considered in the planning process, in the same way that economic and technical criteria are considered. Just as economic and technical requirements may be adapted in the light of experience and changing circumstances, so will the psychological criteria evolve with the system's development.

Criterion	Description
Variation	The need to provide challenge and variation in the work
Development	Enabling employees to learn and develop through the job
Autonomy	Fulfilling the need to make decisions about one's work
Contact	Satisfying the desire for positive social contact and mutual help and support in the work environment and avoiding alienation (see Chapter 7)
Usefulness	The need to know that one's contribution at work is regarded as useful and worthy
Future	Fulfilling the need to see one's job as an integrated part of a satisfying future

Fig. 11.1. Psychological job demands.

A substantial number of workers in modern offices operate some form of VDT such as a word processor screen and keyboard. A great deal of experience of VDTs has been gained from the application of computers in data processing and similar reactions can be identified in office environments. In Chapter 7, Niels Bjørn-Andersen identified job characteristics which could result from computerization:

—some jobs are changed completely (or eliminated);

—there is increased specialization and fragmentation;

—job functions become more routinized;

—less professional skill and experience is required;

—an individual's work is planned and monitored in detail;

—personal contact is reduced;

—work is paced by the computer.

Most of these characteristics arise when there has been a failure in the planning stage to specify psychological and social *(psycho-social)* requirements. The personal impact of such changes on the VDT user's work has often led to symptoms of fatigue, monotony and stress. Increased supervision and monitoring can create great pressures on staff. Coupled with feelings of uncertainty caused by changes in the workplace, this can lead to considerable stress. Changed work procedures entail a change in working rhythm. This demands a period of familiarization and adjustment which may be difficult for someone conditioned to a different work environment.

High-stress jobs

The fragmentation and specialization of jobs will produce varying skills requirements (see Chapter 11). At one end of the scale, there will be relatively few jobs requiring a variety of high skill qualifications. These jobs will include some tasks using VDTs and other electronic office equipment but the prime job functions will have objectives other than operating a computer system. This individual, typically a professional or manager, will be motivated to use computer systems as a 'tool' and is likely to have considerable discretion about when and how to use computing services.

At the other end, there will be more jobs which make simple demands on staff whose prime function is to operate VDTs and other computer systems. These jobs could prove a physical and psychological strain. For example, investigation of a terminal-based data system in an airline booking centre in Stockholm found an increased sense of monotony among operators dealing with seat reservation telephone inquiries from customers.[2] The operators' work was highly specialized — it consisted of only a few individual elements. The scope for planning and self-organization of work was extremely low. Researchers at a Swedish insurance company have found that the stress levels of clerical VDT operators were similar to the levels of bus drivers in the centre of Stockholm during rush hours.[3]

A comprehensive German study[4] also found job dissatisfaction amongst VDT operators. The study covered thirty companies and more than a thousand employees who were engaged in widely varying types of work activities, ranging from simple data recording to jobs which involve a considerable amount of creativity, such as programmers and publishing editors. In data recording jobs, the strongest relationship was found between operators' description of their work as fatiguing on one hand and as trying, frustrating and boring on the other. A very high correlation was found between descriptions of the work as fatiguing and remarks such as: 'My back is strained' and 'I have pains in my neck'. The longer the time spent working at the VDT screen, the more boring, fatiguing and monotonous did the operators find their work. The highest correlation was between the time spent working at the screen and a feeling that all the details of the work were too rigidly defined. Those staff who evaluated their work as 'fatiguing' also showed less satisfaction with their jobs as a whole. The report concluded that, for simple data-recording jobs in particular, there was a combined 'stress' factor determined by the characteristics of job content, work organization, workplace design and the working environment. Although the operators expressed concern with physical symptoms, their responses originated primarily with the highly repetitive nature of the work itself, rather than from the hardware design.

A Swedish study provided strong evidence that the stress reactions among operators depend on the nature of their work and the period of time spent operating the VDT.[5] Johansson and others examined work activities in a Swedish insurance office where several VDTs were interlinked to a control computer. A group of employees carrying out assignments requiring high skills and spending less than half of their working time with VDTs showed the fewest stress reactions. This group regarded VDTs as tools in their work.

The greatest stress levels were registered by groups having comprehensive VDT work involving the input of large amounts of data to the computer system. These operators secreted more adrenalin during work than a control group not working with VDTs and the difference increased after working hours. (The amount of adrenalin is a measure of psychological stress.) The research also showed that high levels of stress were generated when operations were suddenly suspended and when there was a heavy load on the computer and/or telephone network, which caused delays and breaks in service. Accidental stops caused a significant increase in adrenalin levels and feelings of irritation.

Avoiding negative effects
Computer-based systems need not always lead to increases in stress and a deterioration in the working environment. Such negative effects can be overcome if full consideration is given to psycho-social needs in the planning process. In a Norwegian manufacturing company, for example, a production control system was introduced which reduced the stress level on a foreman by removing from him some complex and almost impossible decisions about materials. Negative effects can be avoided if

the system is designed to be flexible and it is adequately appreciated that employee's futures depend on choices made in the selection of the computer system.

The system must be sufficiently flexible to adapt to changes in the environment, job tasks and needs of the user. Inflexible systems are often created because the primary orientation of technical systems designers is towards economic and technical aspects. For example, such designers often stress the importance of 'data discipline', which requires that users are more accurate and precise than previously. This can lead to a rigidity of formats and routines. Such rigidity not only often creates resentment amongst users and clients but can lead to the need to invest a considerable amount of unnecessary money when the system has to be changed or extended. It should be possible to add new functions, remove others, change screen formats, incorporate new instructions and alter transaction methods on a continuously evolving basis.

When the 'fundamental system' is defined, many aspects of job content and organizational methods are also determined. This 'fundamental system' includes the specification of the methods of information processing, software and hardware, manning levels and the basic principles of work organization. At this stage basic psycho-social criteria should be investigated, made explicit, and given priority. When the system is implemented, it should be evaluated in realistic situations to test that it meets its goals.

SOFTWARE FOR THE USER/SYSTEM INTERFACE

A computer-based system can integrate a variety of tasks performed by users with different requirements. In order to cater for these variations, user/system 'interfaces' must be developed to take account of each type of user. Such an interface is, for example, the dialogue carried out at a VDT, with messages presented on the screen and the user responding from the keyboard. Part of the user/system interface relates to hardware ergonomics, as discussed in the previous chapter. Crucial elements of the interface, however, depend on the software.

A system designed for a novice user, for example, would provide a great deal of guidance and progress at a slow pace through the dialogue, with provision for further help if the user does not know what to do next. The interface for a more experienced user can assume a greater degree of expertise and knowledge. The novice user would be confused and intimidated by an interface designed for an expert, while the experienced user would become irritated and frustrated by having to follow an interface designed for a beginner.

The software and systems design therefore needs to be based on an understanding of the user's background and expectations as well as the properties and components of the users' tasks. Guidelines and classifications of the appropriate ergonomics dimensions for the design of interactive computing tasks are less clear cut and quantifiable than for physical ergonomics. A frequent failure in analyzing computer-based tasks is that the focus is often almost exclusively on the expected regularities while those aspects subject to unexpected change and variation are overlooked or underestimated. The consequence may be that users find that the system supports routine tasks, but impedes the performance of informal and unusual activities which frequently arise in offices.

It is more difficult to provide comprehensive and detailed guidelines for interactive dialogue design than it is for physical ergonomics. The following are some principles for designing the software that determines the way communications pass between user and computer system.

Interactive dialogues
A major factor in the user/system interface is the interactive dialogue — the language used to exchange information between the user and the computer. The interaction is controlled by software programmed with the rules and procedures, grammar and syntax of the dialogue language. These languages are far more restricted than natural human languages (for example, English, French, German or Italian), although computer languages do use words from natural languages. The characteristics of the dialogue language, together with the nature of the keyboard, displays and other hardware factors, have a considerable impact on the way a user works.

Figure 11.2 describes some of the main dialogue styles that could be selected. The choice of which style to use is one of the most important decisions made in the course of designing an interactive system. Each style has particular advantages and disadvantages, depending on the user and the task being performed.

Dialogue type	Description
Natural language	The dialogue is conducted in the user's natural language.
Query languages	The user expresses a specific request in the query language and the system produces the appropriate response or report.
Command language	The user initiates actions from a limited, well-defined range of commands.
Function keys	The user indicates desired actions by pressing keys. Each key represents a command or another function.
Menu selection	The user selects one or more actions from a menu list of alternatives presented by the computer.
Form filling	The computer presents a 'form' on a screen with pre-set fields and blank spaces; the user inputs information to 'fill in' the blanks.
Question/ answer	The computer asks a series of questions to which the user responds.

Figure 11.2. Types of interactive dialogues.

Guidelines on dialogue design

The same job tasks can be performed using a variety of different dialogues. In choosing the most appropriate form, an analysis should be made both of the nature of the task being performed and the user's background. For example, a common failing is to provide dialogues that follow a rigid format. The dangers of this are exhibited in a job environment where a clerk needs to respond to the requests of a client or customer by obtaining information from a computer system. If the dialogue is too rigid, the clerk has to impose a sequence of discussion on the client; information provided by the client may be forgotten or misinterpreted if it is given out of the required order. This irritates the client, creates tension in the client/clerk relationship and causes errors and inefficiency. The dialogue should therefore be flexible enough in such a circumstance to enable the user to follow the client's way of asking questions and providing information.

The question of whether the user or the computer has the 'initiative' in a dialogue should be carefully considered. The computer has the initiative in menu, form-filling and question/answer dialogues; in general, this can be useful for systems with inexperienced or occasional users, such as information services accessible to the general public. Sophisticated software with natural language dialogue can be developed for such systems to provide a great deal of subtlety and adaptability in meeting varying human and job needs (see description of expert systems in Chapter 1) but are often the most complex to develop technically. With a user-initiated dialogue, the user generates the required input from his or her memory and the computer produces the necessary responses. These types of dialogue, such as natural or query language tend to assume a degree of expertise on the part of the user. Software can also provide for mixed initiatives, with the dialogue being freely led either by the user or the computer. The question of initiative could be left to the user's own choice by providing a capability for selecting which form is required for a particular purpose.

User profiling

Probably the most important ingredient in software ergonomics is flexibility. Software should aim to have high adaptability, giving the user as many options as possible to tailor the system to specific circumstants; this is sometimes known as *user profiling*. Instead of a designer trying to create a single system which attempts to satisfy all potential users (and often ending up satisfying no one in particular), the user is provided with the tools and options to adapt the general system to a specific task and personal profile.

This can be illustrated by the need to take account of users with different levels of experience. A computer-initiated dialogue, such as a menu system, is suitable for a first-time user. It should be structured in a way which enables such users to learn gradually about the system as they use it. As more knowledge is acquired, however, the computer-initiated dialogue may be insufficient. It may constrain the amount of information conveyed in a single transaction and cause an unacceptable response time.

A system could have to handle users at many different levels of knowledge. One solution is to allow for user profiling. By building more flexibility into the software, users can be encouraged to progress to different levels as their confidence increases. British ergonomist Tom

Stewart has suggested how such a method can be implemented.[6] All first-time users would start with a simple dialogue procedure, involving a combination of menu and form-filling techniques. As experience is gained, the user has the option of over-riding this 'simple' mode by being able to enter information without the need to have to fill-in blanks on a form.

If possible, the user must be capable of controlling the sequence of the dialogue. This is important, for example, in decision-support systems used by managers or in operations where the computer is used to solve problems that arise in an *ad hoc* manner. In these cases, any inflexibility from the computer will be a hindrance to the user.

System response time

The increased use of communications and networked information systems means that many users operate terminals that share processing and storage capabilities with other users. A critical element of performance with such systems is the *response time* — the interval between the completion of a user's input (such as a request for information) and the completion of the computer's response (such as displaying the required information). Long delays on tasks which need a quick response can lead to a decrease in performance and an increase in user dissatisfaction. An excessively varying response time can also be unsatisfactory, particularly for an experienced user. It means that in some circumstances an answer is provided promptly to a complex request that has taken a long time to input, while at other times a short and simple command is followed by a long response time.

Some people imagine that a lengthy waiting time could be an opportunity for a user to have a relaxing pause. Psychological experiments have shown, however, that having initiated a task, a person's energies are mobilized to concentrate on the solution of the task. The person is constantly in a state of 'active waiting'. The wait is particularly disturbing in situations that are typical in computer operations, such as when the break occurs after the nature of the requirement has been firmly outlined by the user, the user has reached 'closure' to a particular step in the problem-solving process, and termination of a particular task component is close at hand.

The user tends to organize activities into *activity blocks,* each consisting of a number of actions which together form a partial segment of the total task. When such an activity block is finished, the user experiences a feeling of temporary satisfaction. If there is excessive or varying response times, the user feels cheated of this satisfying experience. The dissatisfaction of the user will vary according to the nature of the job and task. An occasional user whose main job function is not dependent on receiving a response from the computer system may be prepared to put up with longer responses.

Whatever the circumstances, if there is to be any significant response time, the system should provide feedback messages to inform the user that the computer has accepted the request and that the system is actively working on the problem. If the system has an idea of how long it will take to complete the activity, it could provide a 'count-down clock' to indicate progress. The greatest anxiety to a user can be that the computer system has broken down. If no response is provided, the user may feel the system has 'gone dead'. The provision of temporary feedback messages to let the user know what is happening is therefore an important software ergonomics requirement which assists in the user's job satisfaction.

Microelectronics has greatly improved the processing power of computers but some problems, such as complex scientific calculations, need a considerable amount of time to process. In these cases, a long response is inevitable; the user is often aware that this will happen and so is psychologically prepared to spend time, perhaps performing other tasks while waiting for the answer. Even in this situation, temporary responses should be provided. If the calculations are very long, the temporary response should change to indicate that the calculations are progressing through various identifiable phases.

Just as long delay times can cause psychological and work effectiveness difficulties, so can rapid responses which are too quick for the user. An extremely quick reply can put the user under pressure to respond equally rapidly. The computer is then perceived as a device for pacing the user's work. As a result of this pressure, the user can make errors in trying to respond too quickly and stress and dissatisfaction can increase.

It should be noted that the precise definition of what is 'too quick' or 'too slow' has a significant subjective component. It is therefore difficult to lay down universal standards. Even with similar tasks, users may have different perceptions. This is why a socio-technical approach with user participation and flexible hardware and software provides the most effective way of developing systems to meet the specific requirements of a particular working environment.

Coded and highlighted displays

It is frequently necessary to input and present information as some form of code. In some circumstances, certain information on a display screen may need to be specially highlighted to assist in identifying and searching for information. The coding and display techniques should be developed in the light of the user's experiences and the task requirements.

The best known form of coding in computer systems is the alphanumeric code, consisting of a string of digits and alphabetic characters. Early data-processing systems usually required coding because the cost of computer storage was high, so abbreviated information codes were more economical. These constraints have been alleviated but it is still often necessary, for reasons of user convenience, to continue using the same codes as the earlier systems.

There are two main ways of generating codes — *transformation* and *association*. Transformation codes apply a consistent rule to turn the full information into the codes. For example, the 'country' part of an address may be abbreviated by the rule 'take the first and last letters of the English name of the country'. The transformation codes for Holland, America and England would be HD, AA and ED respectively. An associative code consists of a list which assigns codes to the full information without any standard rule being applied. Associative codes for Holland, America and England, for example, could be CE6, X93 and B47. Associative codes are generally difficult to remember whereas transformation codes can be worked out from the full information and the rule; knowing the rule can also help to work from the code to the full information. Whatever coding method is used, the user should have an efficient means of finding out what the code means, preferably via a 'HELP' facility built into the system or by looking at an easy-to-reference document.

When information is displayed on the screen, various coding techniques can be used in addition to alphanumeric. For example, if there is a colour display, different colours can be used for different categories of information. Shape or 'icon' coding uses symbols to indicate the location of particular types of information. For example, if the system can store voice messages within an electronic mail memo, the point where the message is located can be indicated on the screen by a symbol looking like a microphone or loudspeaker.

Blink coding causes particular information to be flashed on the screen. *Brightness* coding causes some information to be brighter than others.

Other coding techniques include manipulating character sizes, line types (solid or dashed), motion, character distortion and reverse video (such as dark characters on a light background where the rest of the screen has light characters on a dark background). Various display coding techniques should be considered, subject to the availability of the appropriate hardware display capability. The type of technique chosen should depend on the nature of the task. For example, alphanumeric is suitable where it is necessary to provide an absolute identification, such as a password, or product identity number. Colour and shape coding yield good performance in aiding the search and identification of information on a screen. Blink, brightness or reverse video coding is an aid where it is required to target attention on items to be included or excluded. An excessive use of too many or colours or shapes, or an overuse of blinking, reverse video and brightness variations, can cause confusion and strain on the operator.

Information workloads
If there is to be an adequate match between the requirements of the user and the activities of the system, an analysis should be made of how the information workload should be shared between the user and the machine. The human brain has memory and processing/calculating capabilities, but if the user is expected to carry too much or too little of the workload, his or her performance will be adversely affected.

For example, if users are expected to remember too much information, they could make errors or forget crucial aspects. Users should also not be expected to do too much information processing in their head during the interactive dialogue. On the other hand, users will get bored and experience stress if the computer takes over too much of the information load, leaving only boring routine tasks.

The following are some methods that can be used in reducing unnecessary workload demands on the user:[7]

— Use graphic rather than alphanumeric displays to provide easier assimilation of information.

— Ensure the format of the display corresponds to the most important and immediate information needs, eliminating unnecessary data.

— Offer commands with the appropriate capability for the user's immediate task.

— Allow the user to communicate via a natural language or via sufficiently versatile and appropriate commands which minimize demands on the users to rethink or transform their usual working methods.

— Move some clerical operations into the computer, such as using the computer to validate input.

— Make extensive use of *default values*. Many software systems have variables or parameters which can be entered by users to tailor the system to a specific requirement. A default value is that which the system will assume if no value is specified. For example, in an electronic mail system, the list of people who should receive memos from a workstation could have a predefined standard list, which will be the default value unless it is specified that the memos should go to other people or should *not* go to some of those on the list.

VDT operator rest periods

Long periods working at a VDT on routine tasks can create a considerable amount of stress and eye strain. There is therefore general agreement amongst those who have studied the problem that operators should have a rest after a period of continuous work[8] although there is no definition of the optimum duration and frequency of these rests. In technology agreements two hours is generally regarded as the maximum uninterrupted period of VDT work, with shorter times for work that has special visual demands.

Matching systems to users' perceptions

Every user of a system has a subjective mental representation of the task being carried out and the nature of the system with which he or she is confronted. This applies both to the novice and the sophisticated user. An understanding of these perceptions is an important ingredient in making a suitable fit between the user and the system. Messages presented to the users should be in a form consistent with the user's perception of the activity.

For example, if there is an electronic mail facility to store information temporarily before it is deleted from the system, this should be referred to as a 'wastebin' facility and a functional key labelled WASTEBIN could be provided. If, however, this capability was initiated by a command like FILE, STORE or COPY, the user would feel that it is a more permanent store. If the user dialogue and messages are in an inappropriate form, users will transform the information to suit their own internal understanding of the system. This is particularly true of experienced users, who are likely to make assumptions about how the system works. Many errors and misconceptions can arise if there is a mismatch with the user's perceptions, leading to operational inefficiency and operator unhappiness.

The system should also try, as far as possible, to provide *visual integrity* — what you see on the screen is what should appear on the paper. Some word-processor systems, for example, have various codes on the screen interlaced with the typed-in text. This can create confusion in the operator's mind about what the final printed document will look like.

RECOMMENDATIONS

1 Specify psychological and social criteria from the earliest planning stages. These should be used to evaluate the success or failure of the system in operation.

2 Review the psycho-social criteria in the light of experience and changing circumstances.

3 When establishing design goals and specifications consider the need to avoid creating high-stress jobs: they can lead to inefficiency, error, loss of social contacts and alienation (see Chapter 7).

4 Give high priority to ensuring that the system is flexible and adaptable so that individual users can tailor the system to match their own needs.

5 Ergonomics should not be regarded as being concerned exclusively with quantified physical criteria.

6 Consider software and system ergonomic criteria, such as:
   — providing different interfaces and dialogues for various levels of user expertise;
   — matching task and psycho-social needs to the most appropriate interactive dialogue style;
   — ensuring appropriate response times and providing positive feedback where there is a response delay;
   — presenting information on the screen in the best way for particular tasks;
   — sharing the information workload suitably between user and system;
   — fitting the system to users' perceptions of job tasks.

REFERENCES

1 Thorsrud, E., Emery, F.E. *Mot en ny Bedriftsorganisasjon,* Johan Grundt Tanum Forslag, Oslo, 1970.

2 Gunnarsson, E., Östberg, O., Fysisk og Psykisk Arbetsmiljo i ett Terminal Baseret Datasystem, *Undersökningsrapport 1977:35,* Arbetsskyddstyrelsen, Stockholm, 1977.

3 Skandia, *Stress-report,* Stockholm, 1979.

4 Cakir, A., Reuter, H.J., von Schmude, L., Armbruster, A., *Anpassung von Bildschmirmarbeitsplätzen an die physische und psychische Funktionsweise des Menschen,* Bundesminister für Arbeit und Sozialordnung, Bonn, 1978.

5 Johansson, G., Aronsson, G., *Stressreaktioner i Arbete vid Bildskärms Terminal,* Rapporter 27, Psykologiska Institutionen, Stockholm University 1979.

6 Stewart, T.F.M., 'Communicating with Dialogues', *Ergonomics,* Vol 23, No 9, pp 909-919, 1980.

7 Ramsey, H.R., Atwood, M.E., *Human Factors in Computer Systems: A Review of the Literature,* Science Applications Inc., Englewood, CO, 1979.

8 HUSAT Research Group, Loughborough University of Technology, UK, *Health Hazards of VDUs,* John Wiley & Sons, London, 1982.

BIBLIOGRAPHY

Recommended reading of relevance to the issues discussed in this chapter, in addition to the above references, include:

Dainoff, M.J., *Occupational Stress Factors in Secretarial/Clerical Workers,* US Department of Health, Education and Welfare, Public Health Service, Washington DC, 1979.

Damodoran, L., Simpson, A., and Wilson, P., *Designing Systems for People,* National Computing Centre, Manchester, UK, 1980.

Eason, K.D., Damodoran, L., Stewart, T.F.M., *A Survey of Man-computer Interaction in Commercial Applications,* Loughborough University of Technology, Leicestershire, UK, 1974.

Ramsey, H.R., Atwood, M.E., Kirschbaum, P.J., *A Critical Annotated Bibliography of the Literature of Human Factors in Computer Systems,* Science Applications Inc, Englewood, CO, 1979.

CHAPTER 12: TRAINING FOR FUTURE OFFICE SKILLS

Jacques Hebenstreit

INTRODUCTION

This book has shown that computer-based systems will be used by most people who work in offices. Computer systems are also becoming an intrinsic part of many aspects of daily life, with virtually the whole population of industrialized countries using computers in some way. This creates a demand for a wide variety and quickly changing range of new skills.

This chapter examines the educational and training requirements to cope with the new skills that characterize Computer-Assisted Office Work. It examines the nature of these new skills both in the office and in the broader applications of computing in the 'wired society'. The types of people who need to be trained are discussed and the crucial questions of how and where the training can be done are examined. The 'user friendly' ergonomics discussed in Chapters 10 and 11 are shown to be important elements in meeting the educational and training challenge.

THE 'COMPUTER-ASSISTED-X' EXPLOSION

New technologies usually begin in a form which is heavily influenced by the past; cars therefore first looked like coaches and films were regarded as little more than animated photographs. At a later stage, technological progress and social acceptance enable entirely new applications to emerge. Electric engines, for example, were first used only in large equipment to replace steam engines. It took many years before mass-produced electrical equipment became popular. This pattern is being repeated with computing technology.

In their early years, computers grew in size and speed but they were housed mainly in air conditioned cages to which only the 'priests' (the computing specialists) had access, while a large army of 'slaves' fed the retrieval because it is radically different from anyone's practical experiences. The nature of the operational skills needed are defined by the software and hardware capabilities. In addition, training is needed in the general concepts of database management.

Being unaware of the internal structure of a database can be frustrating and inefficient. The result of a query made clumsily or incorrectly by the user can result in the presentation of an unmanageable amount of information which the user cannot refine. The majority of this information could be *information noise* (irrelevant documents) or, even worse, *information silence* — the absence of the most relevant documents, which are in the system, but have not shown up because the query was phrased imprecisely.

An example of the types of new skills needed to gain access to information is the way some query languages use the words 'and' and 'or' in a subtly different way to their everyday meaning. Say a user wants to get a list from a database of the names of all employees and *either* the employee's address *or* phone number and the query language includes the commands LIST OF, AND and OR. If a user requests

LIST OF names AND addresses OR phone numbers

the system might regard the clause 'names AND addresses' as a priority. If the address of an employee is not stored but there is a phone number, the phone number will not be reported to the user. The way of making the enquiry to achieve the user's objective could be to request

LIST OF names AND (addresses OR phone numbers)

Group conferences

Computer-based office information networks offer a wide variety of methods to hold meetings other than requiring participants to travel to the same location (see Chapter 1). In order to ensure that these techniques are used effectively and efficiently, adequate training in interpersonal skills will be required on how to manage the conduct of such meetings.

SKILLS FOR THE 'WIRED' SOCIETY

The activities in the office of the future cannot be isolated from the generalized use of 'Computer-Assisted-X' throughout society, including in the home. Many of the skills necessary for working in offices will be more or less required by everybody. Public viewdata and teletext systems began to make domestic television sets into computer terminals in the late 1970s. Cable networks which carry multiple television channels can also be used for a variety of interactive services. Equipped with an adapted television set and input device, people will have access from home to a variety of 'Computer-Assisted Armchair' activities, including access to up-to-the-minute information, shopping at a distance, handling their own bank accounts, and making airline reservations directly. Electronic mail, facsimile, word processing and personal computing will become as familiar in the home as in offices.

The use of computers will also be intrinsic to the work of all professions, from doctors looking up computer databases on side-effects of drugs to scientists preparing a specialized bibliography, or accountants finding out the latest changes in fiscal law. Computer-Assisted Design (CAD) and Computer-Assisted Manufacturing (CAM) can alter the way goods are created and produced. With CAD, the laborious task of producing detailed design can be eliminated. The designer can engage in a dialogue directly with the system. At each step, the designer can make a decision about how a particular aspect might change and the computer can immediately visualize the impact of the change. If the design seems to be leading to a dead end, starting afresh is relatively easy.

The skills of traditional detailed draughtsmanship and design engineering based on abstract conceptualizations of the results will therefore be less required. The new designers will need to be competent in working with CAD and using its capabilities creatively. In a similar way, CAM introduces the need for new skills in production management. CAM provides systems which allow more factors to be analyzed than could be handled by traditional techniques to assist in making decisions about, for example, the optimal use of machine tools and raw materials.

Although information technology is changing rapidly, it is possible to extrapolate the main trend that will need to be catered for in education and training. The writing of detailed software routines will be left increasingly to a relatively small group of specialists (except for the growing number of enthusiastic amateurs with their own personal computers). The majority of uses will be via an interactive dialogue and the main training requirement will be in the skills needed to accomplish this dialogue. The kinds of user/system dialogues developed (see Chapter 11) and new forms of input and output, such as speech understanding and voice synthesis, will have an impact on the skills training which has to be given.

Most people in offices are already at the limit of their capacity to handle information available to them for their work. Any further load could result in staff being flooded with information. The use of photocopiers to generate duplicates of documents that are often never read is a warning of what could happen with new, more sophisticated information technologies. The proper use of Computer-Assisted Office systems should lead to a decrease in the *flow* of information even though there is an increase in the *volume* of information, i.e. more information will be available but it will go only to where it is needed.

New skills in the office will be needed in three particular areas: communicating information, accessing information and holding group teleconferences.

Information communications activities

Most office communications can be divided into ten main steps: drafting, producing, copying, filing, sending, receiving, filing, retrieving, archiving and destruction. The human skills and resources needed to carry out each of these steps are altered or virtually eliminated by new office technology.

Word and text processing systems make significant changes to the drafting and production phases, both for the 'author' who originates the material, and for the secretary/typist who produces it. With a manual system, the text is usually drafted in handwriting or by dictation. The first draft is typed and checked by the author. It is then retyped and must be checked all through again as new errors may have been introduced during the typing. The author often uses 'cut-and-paste' techniques to rearrange the structure of drafts before getting them retyped. This process continues until there is a satisfactory final form.

A computer-based text editing system, however, makes no real distinction between the first draft and its evolution into the final document. When text is typed in, it is stored in magnetic computer storage, displayed on the screen, and the text is manipulated in this computerized form. Authors need to learn new ways of making changes; 'cut-and-paste' methods become redundant because the typist is manipulating the information as stored, rather than in its printed form. When a change is made, the whole text does not have to be re-read because unchanged text will be left untouched. This alters the whole process of writing and producing documents.

The person operating the computer-based equipment obviously needs to be trained to use it because it has far more potential power and versatility than a manual typewriter and is often more complex to operate. Much of this potential is wasted if the users — authors, secretaries and typists — fail to understand how the system's characteristics can be exploited. It could typically take about twenty days of training for a secretary to completely master a fully computerized text-editing system.

Copying and destroying information become completely different processes when that information is held in electronic, rather than paper, form. A message can be typed into the system once, then sent by electronic mail to as many other terminals in the network as required. Destroying information is a matter of deleting it from the system. The physical copying of documents is likely to involve new equipment, like facsimile transmission. In general, new office technology reduces the need to transport physical documents. Messages, memos, letters, reports, diagrams and pictures can all be transmitted by a single network, which also includes word processors on which text is generated.

New skills are needed to make effective use of electronic mail. Messages need to be expressed concisely. Care must be taken not to misuse the ease with which messages can be sent to a variety of recipients, otherwise each recipient's 'electronic mail box' will be overloaded with unnecessary messages.

Filing and retrieving information
The filing, archiving and retrieval of information represent a major area of changes in skills and techniques. Various computer storage media can be used, such as magnetic disks and tape (see Chapter 1). The main changes, however, involve more than just the physical storage media. In a manual system, filing and retrieval takes place through time, space and various physical cues. 'Get me that document with a red cover which arrived about two weeks ago' or 'The information is in a file in the top drawer of the leftmost filing cabinet' are typical of the way people manage information in traditional offices. Where information is held in computerized storage, however, there are no more time and space references to documents. Everything is organized and filed in abstract structures defined by the kinds of equipment they are on and the Database Management Software employed.

Untrained people have problems in handling computer-based filing and beasts with information. These computers were used essentially as follow-ups to mechanical and electromechanical accounting, calculating and tabulating machines. They could automate and speed up some data-processing tasks previously done by hand, such as calculating and printing payrolls, or processing accounts.

Few people were directly involved in using such computers. The main skill requirements were for the 'priests'. There was also a need for some less skilled staff, such as operators to handle day-to-day machine room needs and data-preparation clerks to create information in coded form on, say, punched cards.

Although the requirements for computing specialists up to the mid-1970s were confined to a relatively small and well defined range of skills, the educational and training system generally failed to adapt quickly enough to the changes. During this period, computing had very little influence on the structure and policy of companies and institutions. In a survey of eight organizations which made intensive use of computer-based information systems, Daniel Robey found that the computing service had caused no changes in formal structures within five organizations.[1] In the other three, the changes caused by computers had usually reinforced the existing structure.

The advent of microelectronics rapidly altered this (see Chapter 1). Cheaper, more compact, more powerful and more versatile systems linked by telecommunications networks made it feasible and affordable to have many computer-based devices in ordinary offices and to have one-person use of systems, like word-processors and personal computers. Computing power could be regarded as more than just a means of automating what had been done in the past. The era of *Computer-Assisted-X* had begun.

Computer-Assisted Office Work
Computer-Assisted Office systems on the market bear the hallmark of the various skill traditions of the manufacturers. There are systems which are oriented towards traditional computer data processing; others resemble office equipment development; some have a bias towards communications techniques. In an equivalent way, many users and technical designers naturally tend towards solutions to those aspects with which they are already familiar. The real requirement, however, is for an integrated, unified approach to providing computer-assisted office systems.

The failure to provide such an integrated approach exacerbates training of users. Incompatible systems which are difficult to operate mean that users have to learn a variety of different complex procedures and that technical designers have to cope with many different technologies and the complexities of interconnecting them. The training problem is further increased because many students leaving schools, colleges and universities have never had a chance of using new computer systems — or may not even have heard of them.

SKILLS FOR THE OFFICE OF THE FUTURE

It is difficult enough to define the skills of the office of today let alone be precise about the skills of an office of the future. In most offices, procedures and techniques have been introduced gradually and new employees often acquire the new skills by a kind of osmosis rather than by real training. New office technology is likely to reduce the need for some traditional office skills (see Chapter 7). On the other hand, there will be a demand for new skills. An important difference between past and future offices has been described by computer scientists D.C. Tsichritzis and F.H. Lochovsky:

> Because of their resilience, people in conventional offices manage to cope in the face of bad design and loosely organized situations. Automated systems usually have much less tolerance for bad design and require much tighter control over organizations and procedures. In an analogy, a small artisan's workshop need not be organized. An assembly line, on the other hand, needs expert organization to function properly. These situations of bad design and loose control will soon manifest themselves in the automated office.[2]

In the past, many activities intrinsic to office work could take place independently of each other. Typewriters could be used to produce text, photocopiers to make duplicates, filing cabinets to store documents, telephone and telex to transmit, receive and disseminate information. Most office equipment could be operated with little or no formal training. With new office technology, however, these activities can be integrated. They can all be activated from the same device linked to a network of computing services. Unless all users are adequately trained to handle the new equipment and the resultant job and organizational changes, efficiency will surely suffer.

Whatever specific techniques are used, a more general trend in basic skills must be catered for. Computing systems tend to increase the proportion of time spent by the user acting on the information produced by computer processing, or monitoring and responding to the work of the computer. The time between making successive decisions becomes shorter as computers take over doing the electronic equivalent of mundane, time consuming 'trivial' tasks like browsing through a filing cabinet to find a document, filling out forms by hand, or adjusting some mechanical parts before producing a machine tool. This means that the user is under more pressure to pay attention to the creative aspects of the job because the periods previously spent in carrying out the 'trivial' parts of tasks were used as a period of intellectual rest.

In order to make the best use of human creativity and computing power, the user should be trained and given responsibility for determining the effectiveness of applying the computing system. The application, therefore, of Taylorism (see Chapter 4) to systems design would be inappropriate because it reduces human responsibility and creativity.

WHO NEEDS TO BE TRAINED?

The previous section illustrated that virtually the whole population will need some form of education and training to be able to make the best use of the variety of readily available new computer-based information services. This requirement is far bigger than the need for skilled computing personnel created in the 1960s.

The first wave of computing in the 1960s and 1970s created a need for systems engineers, project leaders, data processing and computer centre managers, systems analysts, programmers, operators and data preparation clerks. The problem of supplying these specialists was partially solved by adapting curricula in institutional education, with the eventual provision of specific computer science courses. In addition, training has been provided by private institutions and through in-house training by manufacturers, computing service companies and user organizations. Even so, shortages of skilled and experienced computing specialists were still a common problem in many countries in the 1980s. The rapid spread of computing networks, personal computers, word-processors and other computer-based systems creates a skills demand of a much larger and more diverse nature, at a time when the technology itself is changing at an unprecedented rate. Forecasts of the precise

WHERE TRAINING CAN BE DONE

CAL techniques remove many of the traditional constraints on places where education can take place. Special classrooms and educational buildings are no longer the only locations in which to educate and train groups of students. CAL provided on personal computers or through networked information services can be used in the home, offices, factories and other places most convenient to the student, as well as in special educational institutions. Training can take place at times and places convenient to individuals and organizational groups. In offices this helps the efficiency of operations because work patterns need not be suddenly interrupted for a number of individuals to go on a course at the same time, possibly at a long distance from their normal work place.

This does not mean that there will no longer be special educational institutions. There are many valid social and educational reasons why such institutions will be required both in basic schooling and in more advanced specializations at university, college and polytechnic level. Training of computer science specialists, for example, will remain a high level qualification which should be taught in university-level institutions.

Computing is likely to have two major roles in the basic educational system. Firstly, CAL can improve the quality and efficiency of education, provided the software is of an appropriate standard and the systems are introduced with due consideration to their educational, human and organizational consequences.

Secondly, the generalized use of computer-based systems will familiarize all students with the limits and potential of current computing capabilities. This will come about by using computers as an intrinsic part of all disciplines, in arts and humanities as well as science. It will provide familiarity with common basic computing skills and concepts, like simulation, word-processing and databases.

As computers increasingly become a normal feature of all basic education, there will be a decrease in the need for training adults for the 'wired society' and the office of the future. Many of the skills in short supply outlined in this chapter will come to be regarded as common basic skills, as necessary for each person as reading, writing and arithmetic.

RECOMMENDATIONS

For the office of the future

1 Make the transition to new office systems as smooth as possible through gradual change, friendly systems and proper training.

2 Define training requirements that accompany each step of the introduction of new systems for each category of user.

3 Specify training criteria in relation to software ergonomics and the in-built flexibility of the system. New systems should be matched as far as possible to the user's existing experiences and knowledge.

4 Use CAL and audio visual aids as a means of efficiently meeting training needs provided they meet educational, human and organizational criteria, as well as economic and technical objectives.

5 Provide hands-on experience of the new system for training purposes, before the users are expected to work on it in live operation.

6 Systems should include a HELP capability to assist the user and to provide a 'user manual' directly accessible from the computing device.

7 Have a 'consultant', who is also a user and a permanent member of staff, available to advise users, either through personal contact or by being accessible over a computer network.

8 Consult all levels of an organization during systems development, implementation and training programmes. It is only when the objectives of technological changes are clear to everybody, when everybody feels involved and is waiting with curiosity for what is going to happen, that training can really begin.

For education and training institutions

1 Teach the main techniques of using computer-based systems as soon as possible in schools.

2 Regard techniques such as word-processing, electronic filing, electronic mail and database information retrieval as basic skills, taught and used in all subjects and in all levels of the educational and vocational training system.

system has a 'Delete word' key to delete a word, little prior training is needed. Many systems, however, have extremely complex techniques to initiate even simple functions. Procedures like: 'Press Shift and A to delete a word', or something even more complicated, without any obvious relationship to the function, are frequently provided, making it difficult to learn and remember how to operate systems.

The following are some good software and psychological ergonomics principles which can assist to ease the training load in introducing computer-based systems to new users (see also Chapter 11).

— Users should not have to learn complex codes or have to look up technical reference manuals to find out the cause and effect of operational errors.

— The system should explain clearly, in the language of the user, what the error is, its consequences and how these can be checked and fixed. Errors made by users should be 'soft' i.e. they should not cause serious system breakdowns and malfunctions.

— If the user does not know what to do next, a 'HELP' facility should be provided which provides advice and guidance automatically.

— The dialogue between the user and the system should be phrased using vocabulary and a logic that is clearly understandable by the user. The system should have the capability of being 'profiled' to particular needs.

— Whenever a new service is added to a network system, information about the service should be distributed throughout the system in a form which makes them distinguishable from other electronic mail. This information should be in a file accessible to all users and should avoid using technical jargon.

— The existence of a 'consultant' who is one of the users of the system is of great benefit to newcomers or more experienced staff who want to explore advanced uses of the system. For example, in each department, a secretary within that department could become the local word-processing adviser or the adviser could be contacted through a computer network.

— Opportunities should be given for some training to take place using 'hands-on' experience without the user being under the kind of pressure that occurs in live operation.

Computer-Assisted Learning (CAL)

Computer techniques like CAL can be used for self-training and as an aid to teachers. The system presents some information to the student, then asks questions about it. If the student gets the answer correct, the system moves onto the next 'lesson'. If the incorrect answer is given, further information is provided. Progress will be made to the next stage only when the correct answer is given. CAL can therefore be self-paced. The CAL program can monitor the progress of students and provide information to the teacher, who can then personally follow up any particular difficulties.

CAL can be used in conjunction with video tapes and video disks. A portion of video action is shown. Then questions are asked about it and the CAL process continues in a similar fashion to a non-video CAL lesson. The use of CAL with video is sometimes called *interactive video*. CAL aids could be built into systems. Some operator training could therefore be self-taught. CAL software could also be provided on computer networks, accessible from any terminal.

Designing and developing CAL software, however, is a complex and costly process. It requires expertise in the educational aspects of the subject being taught as well as in the technical aspects of the system. The aim of CAL should be to complement rather than replace human teaching. Teachers are needed to deal with specific requirements of individual students and to handle subjects that are not amenable to CAL techniques, which are particularly suited to subjects which involve factual rather than qualitative learning. Having a local 'consultant' who is a user, or access to a user consultant on a network, is an important service to complement any CAL aids.

Great care should be taken in assessing the educational value of CAL systems and the organizational context in which they are introduced. Suitable systems implemented in an appropriate way can be of crucial assistance in filling the teacher-training gap. Despite the high cost of development, CAL systems are generally less expensive than training teachers. They also reduce the numbers of teachers required.

As computer-assisted learning aids will be commonly employed in the future, everyone involved in education will need some training to help them to evaluate and use these new aids effectively. Such systems, called *Computer Assisted Learning (CAL)*, *Computer Assisted Instruction (CAI)* or *Computer Assisted Training (CAT)*, are expected to help solve the enormous problem of the teacher-training gap, as described in the next section.

HOW THE TRAINING CAN BE DONE

The scale of the training problems outlined so far clearly indicates the need for a massive investment in teacher-training, in educational buildings, equipment and in funding students, whether by time off work or through public or private payment of tuition fees. Even if we were willing and able to make the extremely high investments necessary for training, however, there is no guarantee that the results would be effective.

In some aspects, like the training of computing specialists, it might be possible to revise curricula in universities, colleges and polytechnics because it is a relatively limited and self-contained task. The magnitude of the activity needed to train users and teachers is too great to be coped with purely by more investment in traditional training methods. Fortunately, the technology which has created these education and training problems can also offer a solution to them.

Systems for gradual change
In order to ease the transition to new office systems and to keep training needs to manageable proportions, systems should be designed for gradual change, rather than trying to provide the most advanced and futuristic services purely for the sake of being in the vanguard of technical and marketing innovation.

The reason has been explained by Tsichritzis and Lochovsky:

> The organization of most offices evolves over a long period of time. Changes to office procedures or organization are usually introduced gradually. This is because it is fairly difficult, costly and traumatic to reorganize offices continually. Even gradual change can be difficult to

achieve. If new procedures are introduced, then people have to be retrained. If new people are hired, they have to be trained in the current procedures of the office. If new equipment is acquired, office workers have to be trained in its use. Meanwhile, activity in the office should continue as usual without major disruptions to the company's business activities. For these reasons, one is usually very wary of tampering with an office's organization on a large scale. Because of this, the introduction of the automated office has to reflect, initially at least, current office organization and procedures if it is to be successful.[2]

New office systems should therefore have built-in capabilities which allow a smooth transition from the usual way of doing work to an increasingly computer-assisted way. This is achievable through *modularity* in the design. Instead of trying to computerize all aspects at once, particular aspects can be handled by individual modules fit together within an overall design framework, like pieces in a jig-saw puzzle. When the modules are integrated, the system can progress towards a more powerful and comprehensive system.

This approach is important from a psychological point of view. Most people are generally reluctant to employ procedures and equipment which they have never used before. If the new methods and equipment make a sudden change, users can be in a state of perpetual trauma and unhappiness. The result will be that the system is likely to be used inefficiently.

This transition can be eased by designing the systems to take account of human factors. It is possible, for example, to develop computerized filing systems which appear to be analogous with traditional office files. Instead of using the jargon 'database management system', it can be called 'electronic filing'. Instead of talking about database management 'hierarchical or network file organizations', the electronic filing can be structured as 'filing cabinets', with 'drawers' containing 'folders' within which are 'documents'.

If the system is designed with the user in mind, it can be made to be consistent with existing experiences. This reduces training time as well as making the computer seem less frightening and alienating to users.

Friendly systems

An 'unfriendly' system greatly increases the training need because it is so strange to the user's past experience and because many unnecessary details need to be learnt to operate it. For example, if a word processing

3 Make computing systems and services available for hands-on experience in all educational and training institutions.

4 Use educationally-sound CAL to fill the teacher-training gap created by the need to train and retrain whole populations to understand, use and develop new information technologies.

5 Institutions and government departments concerned with education and training should plan to adapt to a new environment where many people will have to be retrained a number of times in their working life and where computers make it possible to deliver effective educational services to the place and at the time most convenient to the student.

REFERENCES

1 Robey, D., 'Computer Information Systems and Organization Structure', *Communications of the ACM,* Vol 24, No 10, pages 679-687, October 1981.

2 Tsichritzis, D.C., Lochovsky, F.H., 'Office Information Systems: The Challenge for the Eighties'. *Proceedings of the IEEE,* Vol 68, No. 9, pages 1054-1059, September 1980.

BIBLIOGRAPHY

Recommended reading of relevance to the issues discussed in this chapter, in addition to the above references, include:

Benbasat, I., Dexter, A.S., Masulis P.S., 'An Experimental Study of the Human/Computer Interface', *Communications of the ACM,* Vol 24, No 11, pages 752-762, November 1981.

Landau, R.M., Bair, J.H., Siegman, J.H., Sandelin, J., *Emerging Office Systems,* Ablex Publishing Corporation, Northwood N.J, 1980.

Naffah, N. (ed), *Integrated Office Systems — Burotics,* Proceedings of the IFIP Workshop, North-Holland, Amsterdam, 1980.

Uhlig, R.P., Forber, D.J., Bair, J.H., *The Office of the Future,* International Council for Computer Communication North-Holland, Amsterdam, 1982.

CHAPTER 13: SOCIAL GOALS IN SYSTEMS PLANNING AND DEVELOPMENT

Rob Kling

INTRODUCTION

This book has shown that the introduction of new office technology has significant social consequences which can alter the lives and social interactions of people working in and serviced by organizations using the systems. Established power structures and management procedures can also be changed. Ultimately a whole organization can become dependent on its automated information technologies to a point where institutional changes cannot be made without first negotiating the web of computing obligations which have to be met before new methods can be introduced.

This chapter summarizes many of the themes developed earlier in the book. An approach is recommended for planning and developing new office systems which incorporates explicit social goals and resolves conflicts between different groups. The main emphasis in the chapter is on large-scale organizations, but the principles examined are applicable to smaller systems and to the research and development undertaken by suppliers of computer-based systems and services.

THE COMPLEXITY OF COMPUTER-BASED INFORMATION SYSTEMS

Many examples have already been given in this book of the diverse nature of applications of new information technologies. Social dimensions of these systems have been illustrated which would be applicable to systems of any size. However, impacts such as 'lost jobs', 'richer workplaces' 'centralization of power', 'increased alienation and stress' and 'loss of personal privacy' increase in significance when more people and groups are influenced by the system and when they are developed by larger organizations.

The automation of a small supermarket in, say, Bonn may affect a few dozen workers, managers and suppliers. On the other hand, if a national government adopts a uniform automated accounting system, hundreds of thousands — even millions — may be affected in offices and organizations around the country. If the supermarket in Bonn reduces staff levels by 20 per cent only a handful of jobs would be lost. If a major public or private organization employing several hundred thousand people reduces its office staffing by 20 per cent, thousands of jobs would be lost to the local clerical labour market.

Is a computer just a 'tool'?
As Jacques Hebenstreit has described in Chapter 12, the 'Computer-Assisted-X' approach provides aids which can be described as *tools* — artifacts which can be used for specific purposes with some discretion and can be replaced when they are unworkable. When the user of a system begins to lose control over what it can be used for and when and how it can be used, it is no longer simply a tool but has broader institutional dimensions.

This is what has happened with larger-scale computing systems. A requirement to modify such a system could involve centralized review, budgetary allocations and research, design, development and testing which may take many years from conception to completion. Such institutional dimensions should be accounted for by planners and others who are evaluating the impacts of new office technology.

Many computer-based systems have been perceived as problematical (see, for example, the case studies and anecdotes in Chapters 2 and 8). They may fail to deliver the benefits of enhanced information processing promised by their advocates and lead to social losses for some participants. Individuals and groups which lose out can further undermine the use of the system in a variety of ways. Even proponents of specific systems may become critical of certain details of the overall design or operation.

A key question to planners and designers of computer-based systems is therefore how to take into account social aspects early enough so that potential problems can be anticipated and minimized. There is no simple and definitive answer but the framework for a desirable approach can be gleaned by examining the analogous task of urban planning in which the social implications have been more explicitly catered for.

Learning lessons from urban planning strategies
Large-scale computer-based information systems are complex artifacts.

So are the transportation systems, neighbourhoods, urban centres and buildings which are the elements of urban planning and development. Computer systems and urban developments are both multi-faceted artifacts for plural, conflicting and not wholly determined uses, where the user/inhabitant is not the designer's direct 'customer'. With urban developments, however, the aesthetics, value choices and political interests are more directly visible.

Just as urban plans shape the social terrain in which we live, computer-based developments form the information habitat and shape the informational terrain of organizations. They both provide new opportunities and sometimes alter the limits of the possible, while simultaneously making life more difficult for some participants. Computer systems designers might do well to consider the roles that urban planners play.

Urban planners and architects accept that functional specifications alone do not determine the effectiveness of an office block or new town centre. They realize that building an actual system calls for additional assumptions about how people will live and work around it. The same is true in creating an electronic mail, inventory control or airline reservation system. As Enid Mumford has shown in Chapter 4, however, computer systems designers have not only failed to consider human and organizational aspects but have often not even been aware that their own technocentric values carry implicit assumptions of how they think people should behave.

One reason why urban planners take more explicit care with the social dimensions of their developments is that built environments are more public and understandable than computer systems. It is easier to analyze and illustrate social aspects of urban developments like New York's Greenwich Village than to assume that people are aware of the operational procedures of the automated budgeting system used by the City of New York.

Most people are aware that, behind the facade of some modern urban developments, many social problems, such as stress, alienation and vandalism, have been fostered because traditional patterns of community support and interaction have been broken. Yet few people are aware of the real working conditions that might lie behind the glamorous facade of a computer-based system. For example, most travellers are familiar with accessing a computerized airline reservation system by personal contact with a travel agent or airport reservation clerk, usually working in comfortable surroundings. The staff who specialize in handling the resultant telephone enquiries, however, could perhaps be working out of sight in highly constrained and monitored working conditions.

Resolving conflicts

In hierarchically structured organizations, executives at the top will have the greatest right to influence the design of the system. Hence, systems designers become technical consultants to senior managers. In this way, designers can reduce the extent to which they get embroiled in social conflicts, leaving it to the authorized manager to allocate resources, resolve differences and mobilize legitimacy for the system. This may work in small organizations but, in many cases, however, there is no single authoritative agent to whom a system planner can turn. New office information systems frequently cut across the boundaries of organizational units which are relatively autonomous, such as divisions in a company, departments in a government or different organizations sharing a common computer service.

The changes caused by new technology can provide benefits to one group in an organization but disadvantages to others. For some managers and staff it may mean an improved working environment and more career potential. For others it may mean a loss of autonomy, more boring and less skilled jobs — or no jobs at all. In these circumstances, the designer must serve plural and sometimes conflicting interests, each with their own power and authority.

Such socially complex and conflict-ridden settings are routine for urban planners. Sometimes urban planners and architects may be preoccupied with short-term, abstract aesthetics, or may be servants of very special interests, but they are often aware that their artefacts have a direct interplay with the kinds of lives that people are encouraged to live within them. The architect Frank Lloyd Wright, for example, sought an organic architecture in which 'it is quite impossible to consider the building as one thing, its furnishing as another and its environment as still another'.[1]

The social web of computing

Many articles about computers for the layman and professional emphasize their role as 'tools', and suggest that organizations are, or should be, relatively unified, task-oriented entities. This gives an imbalanced view of the nature and effects of new information systems, which fails to take account of the actual contours of operational implementations. Information systems can become an organizational web of computing as well as acting as a working tool for some users.[2] Planners must consider how different parties would prefer to integrate use of the system into their local work activity and what constraints its institutional aspects might add.

For example, a budget monitoring system may be viewed as a tool to help managers keep track of expenditures in the subunits under their control. For reasons of efficiency and corporate effectiveness, the system may be shared between many users and organizational units and linked to other computer systems. These sharing arrangements can constrain operational schedules, the procedures for altering the way information is collected and reports presented, or the ways of gaining access to computing resources.

If it is decided to reorganize budget-monitoring, say to identify new cost-centre structures, not only will new software have to be developed, but also changes will have to be agreed and implemented for a complex set of overlapping social obligations in which the computer system is enmeshed. This involves getting appropriate resources, developing and testing the new systems and altering organizational aspects, such as communications channels and reporting arrangements. This can be a cumbersome process because few organizations really do act as a unified entity. Instead they consist, more typically, of rule-oriented bureaucracies with competing sets of political fiefdoms.

Another way in which the web of computing can impose possibly undesirable conditions on parts of the organization is in the selection of systems and software from vendors. For example, if the Finance Director decides to choose a computer because it has good accounting software, other managers and staff will have to make do with software available on that computer, even if it is inadequate for their own needs. Some organizations may decide to standardize on a particular software system but then may have to go to considerable expense and spend a long time tailoring it to the particular needs of some units.

CRITERIA FOR EVALUATING SOCIAL IMPACT OF COMPUTER SYSTEMS

Urban planners who want to make a responsible assessment of the social impact of, say, the location of an airport, can draw on a generally agreed set of criteria and be reasonably sure of having covered the most important aspects. Noise, pollution, job creation, accident risks and ground transport access (with its own associated social and environmental consequences) are some of the aspects that will be considered. Computer-based office information systems, however, are still a relatively new phenomenon. The rapid growth and innovation of systems using microelectronics makes it difficult to examine relatively stable implementations.

Systems planners and designers need some framework in which to proceed even if, subsequently, different emphases are assumed or new ones are introduced. This book has provided such guidelines in many areas. These can be encompassed within thirteen important social dimensions: quality of life; social fabric of group life; power and control; dependency on specialized resources; intelligibility of arrangements; employment patterns; privacy; organizational and technical fit; infrastructural demands; equity in sharing benefits and costs; ideology; accountability; and social carrying costs.

Rarely can one say with certainty that any of these factors will be influenced in a particular direction by 'more computing'. There are many possible outcomes which hinge on differences of design and implementation strategies, internal pricing of operations, and the overall environment. Some computer systems, for example, support increased centralization of power and control, others assist more decentralized operations. New office technology can enrich jobs or can 'make' jobs more fragmented, routine and monotonous. Systems have to be designed to make the many trade-offs necessary to meet the pluralistic needs of users so it is impossible to specify a standard profile of likely impacts.

The next section proposes a planning strategy which emphasizes the continual review of designs and operations to monitor their effect on social and organizational life. First, the thirteen social dimensions will be discussed. Note that the constituencies served by a particular system will have differing views on the importance of each dimension and that other dimensions could be added.

1 *The quality of life.* This diffuse concept has been most carefully examined within organizations in terms of 'the quality of working environment'. The impact of computerization on public life in general has been less thoroughly analyzed, but is equally important in determining the overall quality of life in a society with widespread use of computer-based systems. The arguments put forward in favour of computerization tend to view 'the good life' as one which is lived with zealous and cheerful efficiency. There is more to the quality of life, however, than the simple material forms of convenience and flexibility which are the usual basis of justification for specific computing applications.

2 *Social fabric of group life.* 'Social fabric' is a metaphor for the ways that people interact and the norms that guide their behaviour. It is related to the 'quality of working environment' and 'quality of life' but is concerned specifically with the kind of moral order, social patterns, and 'office cultures' which characterize daily life. The social fabric of offices using computing intensively will be substantially different to worklife in traditional offices. For example, in some professional offices, extensive use will be made of home-based work and electronic mail so staff will see less of each other physically. In other offices, however, clerical staff may be far more regimented in their working life than in non-computerized offices.

3 *Power and control.* As Michel Crozier and Brian Wynne have explained in Chapters 5 and 8, computer-based information systems can alter the distribution of power within organizations. This is caused by the new ways in which information is channelled via the system. Users also become dependent on other organizational (sub)units for critical computing resources. The finding of one in-depth study of the impact of computing systems on power relationships concluded that computer systems are often employed to reinforce the power of organizational elites.[3]

4 *Dependency on specialized resources and suppliers.* Organizations which completely replace manual systems with computer-based ones can become dependent on this powerful and complex technology, on the supply of technical experts to develop and maintain it, on outside suppliers of equipment and services, and on continuing funding to support and channel the technology. This dependency can be decreased by, for example, having a great deal of local participation in designing the system, by selecting hardware and software that can be obtained from many sources and by ensuring that the system

is sufficiently reliable to avoid significant breaks in the availability of the computing service.

5 *Intelligibility of social and technical arrangements.* An important humanistic goal is to try to ensure that most people can comprehend the social and technical worlds in which they live. Everyone does not, however, have the time to learn the fine-grained detail of 'how things work'. Users and clients who are dependent on computer-based systems should still understand four key aspects relating to: data, errors, procedures and communications. The kinds of data stored, the structure of databases and means of accessing them should be clear. Error detection should unambiguously and intelligibly report the cause of a fault and how it can be corrected (if it cannot be fixed automatically). The procedures and processes of the computer system should be comprehensible but must not obscure the organization's processes. Communications from the system should be explicit about the actions being taken in relation to the user or client both during normal operation and in response to errors.

6 *Employment patterns.* Computer-based systems alter the mix of skills required in industry, commerce, public administrations and health and welfare services. They can eliminate some jobs altogether and create new ones (see Chapter 9). In a period of growth, labour savings are masked by economic expansion. Stagnation and recession, however, could accentuate the loss of jobs caused by technology, at least in the short-term. A careful analysis of the employment implications of new office technology should be made for each project, as well as being considered in international, national and regional policies.

7 *Privacy.* The terms 'privacy' or 'data protection' are used to indicate the extent to which a person can control the collection of data about oneself, and who can access and manipulate that information. While a great deal of concern has been expressed about the use of computerized records of public bodies, many employees expect specific privacy guarantees at the workplace, for example, as clauses in technology agreements (see Chapter 9). Many countries have data protection legislation to provide general guidelines and mechanisms, such as independent Data Protection Authorities, to monitor and implement legal requirements.

8 *Fit between computing arrangements and social/organizational culture.* The 'fit' of a system is the extent to which the procedural demands made by new office technology align with the practices of its host organization. Misfits can occur when the technology imposes new 'cultural' norms, for example when a highly analytical computing method is used to support decision making in an organization that has traditionally succeeded through intuitive judgements and extended intergroup negotiations.

9 *Infrastructural demands.* The 'infrastructure' covers those resources which are needed to support provision of the computer-based service, such as skilled staff, good operations procedures, stable electrical power, effective telecommunications lines and an appropriate physical working environment (see Chapter 10). These infrastructural resources are often underestimated, taken for granted or cut back when economizing becomes necessary because they have no immediate and tangible payoff. Like preventive maintenance of capital equipment, however, the costs of skimping are likely to become more apparent in the long run.

10 *Equity in receiving benefits and bearing costs.* As I discussed earlier in drawing an analogy with urban planning, computer-based systems must satisfy pluralistic communities in which new developments will have different benefit/cost balances for different groups and individuals. The achievement of equity, or fairness, is regarded as an important aim in many societies. Where equity is not perceived to exist, conflicts will occur which could be resolved by co-operative negotiation, say via labour-relations bargaining, or by even more divisive means. Such fairness needs to be considered both within specific workplaces and in society in general. Some partisans of computer systems view them as vehicles to engineer larger organizational or social changes, but such attempts can be regarded as troublesome intrusions by those groups which value the existing arrangements.

11 *Ideology.* Ideologies are relatively well integrated systems of belief about what is important in the world and how people and social groups should act. Enid Mumford in Chapter 4 described two distinct ideologies which have influenced designs of computer-based systems – scientific management and socio-technical. As she explained, the ideological assumptions of 'Taylorism' are often implicit in the approach of technical systems designers. The ideology underlying

the systems design is a critical determinant of what the system 'means'.

12   *Social accountability.* The extent to which users and clients are well or poorly served by computer-based information systems — and the degree to which they can influence the developers and operators of the system — are defined in terms of a social accountability, which goes beyond purely economic or technical criteria and assessments. Several social arrangements have been relied on to implement such accountability, such as legal contracts, professional standards, administrative authority and the mechanisms of free-enterprise competitive markets. Although these can be applied to computing systems, they have severe limitations. An important practical design consideration is to decide how effective social accountability can be implemented.

13   *Social carrying costs.* The direct or indirect costs borne by third parties or the general public which accrue throughout the life of a project should be evaluated as social carrying costs.[4] For heavy industrial developments, these include environmental pollution and the costs of accidents and injury to workers. There are complementary social benefits, such as a cleaner physical environment and safer industries. The assessment of the social carrying costs of new office technology encompasses the issues discussed in the previous twelve social criteria. It should not be regarded as a purely quantitative exercise, say by trying to compare the numbers of jobs created and destroyed by the technology. Rather, it should encourage key participants to identify and discuss the net sum of social costs and benefits throughout the life cycle of the system.

A STRATEGY FOR COMPUTER SYSTEM PLANNING AND DESIGN

The planning and design of computer-based systems is often dominated by specifications of technical and functional capabilities. It is easier to focus on the exciting and concrete information handling capabilities of new equipment than on the much less tangible and more diffuse social impacts of deploying the equipment.

Equipment is something that can be conceptualized, specified, purchased and installed by action-oriented participants; it can spew out reports and flash interesting and colourful displays. People, forms and reports can be relatively easily organized, moved and otherwise acted on. In contrast, social impacts are usually less directly actionable. They may be by-products of a complex series of activities, as well as of social forces which are well outside the direct control of the planners, designers, workers and managers who participate in systems design.

Larger computer-based systems evolve as their users, clients, operators and others begin to understand their opportunities, demands and constraints. It is difficult to forecast change for the more quantifiable elements in the systems, such as the equipment, let alone the more intangible social impacts. Pro-social planning is a fragile process, particularly in relation to information technology developments where the 'evidence' is less visible and where there is a much shorter history of experience than in urban planning. This is exacerbated by the explosive technological innovation across a broad range of computer-based equipment and services. Yet hope and luck are the only alternatives to a systematic attempt to plan for social as well as technical and economic aspects.

By extracting relevant lessons from the experiences of urban planners, however, it *is* possible to design and develop computer-based systems with a ten to twenty-year life span which should avoid large mistakes and satisfy many of the social dimensions specified in the previous section. To do this, planners should consider their designs as being in continual evolution, specify explicit social goals, treat designs as experiments, and institutionalize good design reviews.

A six-stage strategy
The following are six main stages in planning and developing computer-based information systems which suggest a methodology for creating computer-based 'information environments', which will be attractive for users and other participants to live with.

1 *Develop a social and functional plan.* The most effective strategy for meeting the many social and functional needs is to have a clear, operationally-oriented plan, which specifies the values to be emphasized or left intact by specific technical plans. Then inevitable proposals for alterations can be reviewed in the context of the plan, in a way which maintains important social goals by balanced adjustments. Otherwise, social objectives can be undermined through a sequence of relatively minor technical and other changes. This approach, developed in urban planning,[5] is equally applicable to

computer-based systems. These could be useless or counterproductive, however, if there is a mishandling of the development of the guiding plan, of those who administer it, of what it covers and of the detail in which it is specified (see Chapter 3). Developing a plan should be seen as an opportunity to build consensus rather than as an exercise in creating a vague policy statement which hides the real intentions of particular power groups.

2 *Examine institutional as well as functional feasibility and appropriateness.* The feasibility of a new office technology project is as much dependent on the availability of appropriate organizational resources as on having the technical systems to perform the required auto-mated functions. An important organizational resource, for example, is having staff with the skills needed to negotiate contracts with vendors, as well as being able to design and implement systems.

3 *Involve a diverse and 'representative' group in the planning, design and implementation reviews.* There are two main ways of developing systems. Either a team is authorized by a special 'sponsoring' interest or else lay people in the organization agree to involve a diverse range of users and participants. The 'authorized team' method is likely to mean the system is most sharply aimed at the interests of the sponsoring group (although other groups may try to undermine it). Enid Mumford in Chapter 4 explained the main advantages put forward by proponents of participation — the achievement of a system tuned to real social and technical needs, increased acceptability to users and the satisfying of a desirable democratic value. There is some evidence from urban planning to support this view,[5] provided an adequate 'political architecture' has been developed to decide the most appropriate answers to the questions of who should be involved, how, and with what power.

4 *Continue design and implementation reviews through the system's life cycle.* In the 1970s, some software engineering theorists and systems analysts conceptualized the life history of a computer-based information system as a linear sequence of successive stages such as require-ments specification, design, coding, testing, training, documenta-tion and maintenance. Michel Crozier in Chapter 5, however, explained why systems development should proceed as a circular, iterative process. Most systems are under continuing renovation. In order to be kept 'on course' for the original social, technical and economic goals, systematic design reviews are needed during the life

of the system rather than terminating reviews when the system becomes operational. Such reviews should avoid bureaucratizing organizational and equipment changes. The effectiveness of the reviews depends on having updated and workable plans, skilled reviewers, realistic feedback from the operators of the systems and the co-operation of those who can authorize any necessary changes.

5 *Evaluate the potential social impacts of different design solutions.* There is no simple formula for evaluating how a particular computer-based information system will affect the thirteen social dimensions identified earlier. In order to gain insight into how to create a 'habitable information environment', planners should take three main actions. First, they should develop an intimate appreciation, through selective interviews and direct observations,[6] of the work worlds of potential users, operations staff and organizational clients. Second, planners should develop rich and varied scenarios about the *actual* use and evolution of the system as it is likely to be experienced by different participants. Third, they should use the rapid creation of prototypes of aspects of the system to get early feedback about the 'habitability' of systems components; such prototypes must be integrated into the real operational environment to give a true perception of the 'system-as-experienced'.

6 *Maintain the adaptability of the system through incremental design and implementation.* The unpredictability of the social and technical aspects of computerized systems makes it desirable to avoid major traumas by implementing technical and organizational strategies which allowsubstantial flexibility and are not impossible to reverse should extreme difficulties occur. Such strategies have costs as well as benefits. For example, additional investment is needed to overcome the losses of economy in scale gained by being able to deploy many similar small units rather than encouraging diversity. A diverse strategyalso takes longer to develop and implement than astandardized solution.

IMPLICATIONS FOR EQUIPMENT RESEARCH AND DEVELOPMENT

This chapter has focused on large-scale implementations of computer-based information systems and has provided guidelines to the planners and implementors of such systems. In order to achieve their social and technical aims, they need to have at their disposal appropriate equipment and systems incorporating, for example, suitable flexibility, good physical ergonomic design and 'user friendly' interactions, just as urban planners need appropriate building equipment and transportation systems to turn their conceptions into reality.

Computer equipment and software are more than just 'dumb' bricks in a wall. The software controlling user/system interactions, for example, is not just an item to be used. It actively shapes the way its operator carries out his or her job, including the sequence of job tasks. The kinds of systems offered by vendors are therefore of crucial significance in enabling designers to meet social goals.

Prime values of vendors are to improve their profits and to maintain market share through competitiveness. Organizations implementing computer systems also usually regard the minimizing of capital outlay as an important requirement. The result is that human factors and social values are lost in trade-offs against costs, unless there is an explicit appreciation of the importance of the social dimensions. The cheapest system designs tend to minimize costs by, for example, eliminating important cues on the display screens, shortening and therefore reducing the comprehensibility of messages in interactive dialogues, and having limited features for the detection, reporting and correction of errors. Operational costs can be further reduced by designing programs which increase machine efficiency by sacrificing flexibility in user interactions and in the system's adaptability to suit different social values.

Just as pressure from government agencies, consumer and other interest groups has raised awareness of health and safety requirements in other industries, so have laws, users and unions influenced computer vendors. For example, the combination of government legislation and union demands for improved ergonomics in Scandinavia and West Germany have played a major role in causing computer and office automation manufacturers to incorporate some recommended physical ergonomic guidelines in their systems.

The relevance of the human and organizational aspects described in this chapter, and the book as a whole, should make vendors as well as users realize that the ultimate effectiveness of new office technology depends on satisfying pro-social goals. In the long run, vendors will be asked to produce capabilities which satisfy users' needs for 'friendly' systems, i.e. support varied social arrangements, good physical ergonomics, low social carrying costs, and so on.

Vendors' research and development should therefore include such considerations from the initial conception of projects. Human factors engineers, ergonomists and sociologists should be involved in the design at the start. If, as frequently happens, they are called in as consultants at a late stage in development, their influence can only be marginal. The costs of re-orienting the system to better ergonomic guidelines at a later stage will be far higher than if they had been built into the initial design. The testing and assessment of equipment should take place in user environments of a realistic organization scale rather than only in specialized individually-oriented laboratory conditions, or with 'tame' existing users, who may be untypical of general user environments. The guidelines and recommendations in Chapters 10 and 11 should be considered by vendors in their research and development strategies.

RECOMMENDATIONS

1 Regard the development of computer-based information systems as a complex planning and development project which aims to provide an 'information habitat' acceptable to a pluralistic user and client community.

2 Approach planning and development in an appropriate systematic manner, which explicitly considers social as well as technical and economic goals.

3 Establish the social dimensions which will be used in assessing the behaviour of the operational system. Thirteen dimensions have been suggested as a starting point: quality of life; social fabric; power and control; dependency on specialist resources; intelligibility of social and technical arrangements; employment patterns; privacy; organizational fit; infrastructural demands; equity in sharing costs and benefits; ideology; social accountability; and social carrying costs.

4 Implement a systematic planning and development strategy. Six key steps in such a strategy have been suggested:

— develop a social and functional plan;
— examine institutional as well as functional feasibility;
— involve a diverse and representative group of participants;
— continue design and review through the life-span of the system;
— evaluate social impacts of different design solutions;
— maintain the adaptability of the system.

5 Vendors should incorporate social goals from the very beginning of their research and development programs.

Rob Kling would like to acknowledge the assistance of Ray Catalano, Joe DiMento, Les Gasser, Suzi Iacono and Rob Rittenhouse in discussing this chapter during its drafting.

REFERENCES

1 Jencks, C., *Modern Movements in Architecture*, Doubleday, New York, 1973.

2 Kling, R., Scacchi, W., 'The Web of Computing: Computer Technology as Social Organization', *Advances in Computers*, Vol 21, Academic Press, New York, 1982.

3 Danziger, J., Dutton, W., Kling, R., Kraemer, K., *Computers and Politics: High Technology in American Local Governments*, Columbia University Press, New York, 1982.

4 Kapp, K.W., *The Social Costs of Private Enterprise*, Schocken Books, New York, 1971.

5 DiMento, J. F., *The Consistency Controvesy and the Limits of Planning*, Oelgeschlager, Gunn & Hain, Cambridge MA, 1980.

6 Lofland, J., *Analyzing Social Settings*, Wadsworth Publishing, Belmont, CA (1971) and Spradley, J.P., *Participant Observation*, Holt, Rhinehart and Winston, New York, 1980.

BIBLIOGRAPHY

Recommended reading of relevance to the issues discussed in this chapter, in addition to the above references, include:

Collingridge, D., *The Social Control of Technology*, Frances Pinter, London, 1980.

Forester, T. (ed), *The Microelectronics Revolution*, Basil Blackwell, Oxford, UK, 1980, and MIT Cambridge MA, 1981.

Goodman, Paul, Goodman Percival, *Communitas: Means of Livelihood and Ways of Life,* Random House, New York, 1960.

King, J.L., Kraemer, K.L., 'Cost as a Social Impact of Computing' in Moss, M. (ed), *Telecommunications and Productivity*, Addison-Wesley, Reading MA, 1981.

Kling, R., 'Social Analysis of Computing: Recent Empirical Research', *Computing Surveys*, Vol 12, No 1, pages 61-110, March 1980.

Lucas, H.C. *Why Information Systems Fail*, Columbia University Pres, New York, 1972.

Pressman, R.S. *Software Engineering: A Practitioner's Approach*, McGraw-Hill, New York, 1982.

Index